FRUIT PURSUIT

A Deeper Look into Galatians 5

HANNAH BETH BROWN

© 2025 Hannah Beth Brown

Cover, illustrations, and interior layout designed by Christie Canova Carey

All rights reserved. No part of this publication may be reproduced, stored in a retrieval system, or transmitted in any form or by any means—electronic, mechanical, photocopying, recording, or otherwise— without prior written permission.

IBSN: 979-8-218-58072-8

Printed in the United States of America

Webster, Noah. "Dictionary by Merriam-Webster: America's Most-Trusted Online Dictionary." Merriam-Webster, Merriam-Webster, 1996, www.merriam-webster.com/.

Scripture quotations marked (ESV) are taken from ESV® Bible The Holy Bible, English Standard Version® ESV® Text Edition: 2016. Copyright © 2001 by Crossway, a publishing ministry of Good News Publishers. The ESV® text has been reproduced in cooperation with and by permission of Good News Publishers. Unauthorized reproduction of this publication is prohibited. All rights reserved.

Scripture quotations marked (NIV) are taken from the Holy Bible, New International Version®, NIV®. Copyright © 1973, 1978, 1984, 2011 by Biblica, Inc.™ Used by permission of Zondervan. All rights reserved worldwide. www.zondervan.com The "NIV" and "New International Version" are trademarks registered in the United States Patent and Trademark Office by Biblica, Inc.

Scripture quotations marked (NLT) are taken from the Holy Bible, New Living Translation, copyright ©1996, 2004, 2015 by Tyndale House Foundation. Used by permission of Tyndale House Publishers, Carol Stream, Illinois 60188. All rights reserved.

THIS BOOK IS DEDICATED TO
MY NINA AND MY NANA.

MY GRANDMOTHERS, FAYE HINSON AND JOSETTE BROWN, SO BEAUTIFULLY DEMONSTRATED THE FRUIT OF THE SPIRIT WITHIN THEIR LIVES.

Table of Contents

FOREWORD — 1

INTRODUCTION: ABUNDANTLY OVERWHELMED — 3

CHAPTER 1: OVERWHELMINGLY ABUNDANT — 9

CHAPTER 2: LOVE — 22

CHAPTER 3: JOY — 31

CHAPTER 4: PEACE — 40

CHAPTER 5: PATIENCE — 49

CHAPTER 6: KINDNESS — 57

CHAPTER 7: GOODNESS — 65

CHAPTER 8: FAITHFULNESS — 73

CHAPTER 9: GENTLENESS — 81

CHAPTER 10: SELF-CONTROL — 90

CHAPTER 11: FRUIT NOURISHES — 98

CHAPTER 12: KEEP PRESSING — 104

ENDNOTES — 108

ALL MY THANKS — 109

ABOUT THE AUTHOR — 111

FOREWORD

Fruit in the Life of Jesus

EVERY DAY DISCIPLE

"If you are lacking **LOVE**, listen again to the prayerful tears of Christ that watered the soil of Gethsemane so that he just might make it to the cross to be able to die for a world that rejected Him. Listen closely if maybe you might hear your name on His lips or your neighbor's name, or your enemy's. If it has been a while since you have experienced **JOY**, may I commend to you the man on trial, whose friends had abandoned Him, disciples denied Him, false witnesses accused Him, and evil leaders convicted Him, and STILL He stood silent knowing that the joy set before Him was greater than the fear circling around Him. If **PEACE** seems to be escaping you, draw near to the man being beaten with the lash. And even as each swing of the soldier's arm tore through His flesh exposing muscle and bone, He remained silent, even compassionate. A true peace that surpasses all understanding. If you have trouble walking in **PATIENCE**, circle around with a crowd screaming at a man carrying His own cross. Be in awe that your voice seems to be among them. See how they mock Him, belittle Him, spit on Him, and slap Him across the face, and he only takes the time to readjust the splintered beam on His shoulder so that He may keep on moving forward. If you need a cue for **KINDNESS**, hear His prayer spoken over the ones who had just struck a nail the size of a railroad spike into

Foreword

His hands, shaking His entire scarred body as they drove yet another one His feet. Notice the words falling to the ground like a refreshing rain, "Father forgive them, for they don't know what they are doing." If it is hard to glimpse **GOODNESS** in a world gone crazy, reflect upon the revelation of a war-battered centurion who looked upon this mangled man and yet saw the most pure essence of goodness he had ever witnessed, causing him to declare, "Surely, this man was the Son of God." If you are weary of a lack of **FAITHFULNESS**, gaze upon a man who would even use what final strength He had left to lift up His broken body, filling His labored lungs for one final faithful prayer, "Father, into your hands I commit my spirit." If you have forgotten the touch of **GENTLENESS**, see how gently Christ's female disciples and Joseph of Arimethea take down their rabbi's unrecognizable body from the cross wrapping Him in burial clothes, and laying Him in a hollowed-out tomb. And if you have looked down on the true power of **SELF-CONTROL**, just wait around three days as that same unrecognizable, martyred teacher walks out of the tomb in glorious, radiant, resurrected beauty and see if His words don't echo in your head, "NO ONE takes my life from me! For I have the power to lay it down and I have the power to take it up again!"

– Meredith Knox, Teaching Pastor at New Spring Church, Excerpt from her message titled, "Every Day Disciple" from January 26th, 2025

INTRODUCTION
Abundantly Overwhelmed

"And God is able to make all grace abound to you, so that having sufficiency in all things at all times, you may abound in every good work." — 2 Corinthians 9:8 (NIV)

Have you ever felt God overwhelm you with His abundant grace at the perfect time? I am thankful I have experienced this on several occasions, but on one particular instance in college I experienced a moment of God's grace that I will never forget. During my fall semester of junior year, I sat down to decide which classes I needed to take in the spring semester. I stared at the list of classes I had left to take before graduation and felt really overwhelmed. I was nearing the end of my college career, and I knew the remaining three semesters would fly by as fast as the previous five semesters. My mind began to wander beyond my academic load toward my other commitments. I was not only double majoring, but I was working as a student ambassador for my school, encouraging a group of freshman students, and leading a Bible study. I was also prioritizing many relationships in my life. I was doing my best to balance time with family, roommates, and friends. I felt as though I was barely taking time to take care of myself. The time I allotted each week to exercise grew smaller, I wasn't sleeping as much, and my time with the Lord became shorter. It was as if all of a sudden my eyes were opened to the life I was truly living.

Introduction

In this moment during my junior year, I realized that for as long as I can remember, I have bounced from one activity to the next with barely enough time to catch my breath in between. I was saying yes to so many opportunities that my schedule became overwhelmingly full. I found myself multitasking in class to complete all my responsibilities, half-listening to a friend as I scrambled to finish a homework assignment, or having to cut short an important conversation due to another obligation. Most days, I felt like a chicken running around with my head cut off. I know that sounds silly, but there were days when I would literally run from the building where I worked on campus to my next class so that I wouldn't be late. I am someone who loves to use a planner to stay organized, but this particular semester, my planner looked everything but organized. I could tell by the scribbles and scratches everywhere in my planner that my life was too busy. I desperately needed to slow down. I began to notice this physically because my body was tired, my brain was exhausted, and even though I love people, some days I just wanted to be alone. When I sat down to navigate my spring semester class schedule, it was like God sent a shockwave of awareness to me. I was living life at a breakneck pace. I felt overwhelmed almost all the time. I didn't know how to communicate this feeling to other people because most college students are also really busy. However, saying that my life was busy is an understatement. My full schedule led me to depletion. Trying to keep up with this schedule left me feeling exhausted.

After God helped me realize that the pace of my life was unhealthy, I knew I needed to implement habits to slow down, but I had no idea where to start. I am someone who enjoys being busy, but this amount of busyness was too much. I knew I needed to say no to some opportunities and prioritize the areas of my life that mattered the most. With God's help, I have learned the value of resting and slowing down, but this is a journey I am still navigating. My natural tendency is to multitask, do it all, and say yes to everything. As a people-pleaser with a fear of disappointing others, this was the routine I found myself slipping into day in and day out. During this season of busyness, I believed that the more I was involved in, the more fruit God could produce in me. However, God began to teach me that the truth in His Word says quite the opposite. God does produce fruit in our lives, but if we become too overwhelmed, we begin to produce a different kind of fruit.

God began to teach me that bearing fruit does not depend on how many accomplishments I earn, how many relationships I have, or the number of areas I am devoted toward. Instead, fruit comes from abiding and resting in God's presence. I was letting hurry dominate my schedule to the point of missing God's presence in my daily life. Once I realized the way I was living, my heart felt relieved. I honestly don't know how I was surviving living life at such a busy pace. I loved the areas I was involved in, but it became too large for me to handle all at once. I felt as though I was looking at a ten-foot wave about to crash down on top of me. I don't want to go back to living a life of hurry. Now, I can clearly see God's immense patience with me as I rushed past Him and chose to hurry through life. My relationship with God suffered because I prioritized busyness and failed to slow down. I think back to several other moments, areas, and relationships in my life that suffered due to my habit of hurrying. Busyness and hurry go hand in hand because when our schedule becomes too busy, our lives become filled with hurry. This is not the kind of life Jesus desires for us. Instead, God began to teach me that He wanted me to slow down, be still, and practice the act of being present. I began to learn the significance of abiding by practicing presence. I recognized in John 15 that God attaches a beautiful promise to abiding: that we will bear much fruit. God helped me realize that I needed to revisit the idea of bearing fruit before I could truly understand the concept of abiding in Him. I wanted to discover what it looked like to rest and abide in God's presence.

LEARNING TO ABIDE

Since this moment during my junior year, God has been teaching me that any kind of hurry removes the possibility of growth because growing takes time. In my state of busyness and hurry, I stopped bearing fruit. Growth was not happening within my spiritual life because I was not abiding or resting. We have the choice to be busy and hurry or abide and rest. Which one do you desire? I desired a life of abiding and resting, but was trying to achieve that lifestyle through busyness and hurry. I eventually discovered that such a life only leads to exhaustion and disappointment. However, a life of abiding and resting leads to fruitfulness and abundance. I needed to realize that a fast-paced life is not what Jesus intends for His people. In fact, Jesus demonstrates a very slow-paced life. Jesus allows for interruptions many times in Scripture, and these moments serve as some of the greatest ministry opportunities for Him. I began to pray asking for God's help because I wanted to live life like Jesus and I knew that this meant I needed to learn how to abide in Him. In his book *Practicing the Way*, John Mark Comer notes that, "The question isn't, Are you abiding? It's, What are you abiding in?"[1] We all abide. Take some time now to reflect on what or in whom you are abiding. Is it the aim of perfection? Is it your family, friends, or significant other? Is it your never-ending list of responsibilities? Let's devote ourselves to abiding in God's presence together.

I wrote a prayer to voice my thoughts to the Lord on October 27th, 2023 that says, "Dear Lord, I just need to be honest. I feel stretched way too thin…I feel depleted, and I don't know what to do from here." Here are some more notes from October 2023 about the ways I felt:

"I am doing my best, but it doesn't seem like enough."

"I sometimes feel like a failure."

"I highly dislike disappointing people."

"I have a tendency to fall into people-pleasing."

"I have a fear of living an insignificant life."

"I feel like I have no time to rest even though I sense that I need it."

"I feel like I am barely getting by…hanging on…keeping up."

"I feel drained, discouraged, and defeated."

"I feel like I have to be everywhere for everyone."

"I do not want to be a burden to anyone."

"I feel overwhelmed a lot."

Do any of these thoughts resonate with you? In November of 2023, God began teaching me and answering these prayers. Here are some glimpses:

"God, help me be honest." (11/02)

"God, please forgive me for living a hurried life." (11/03)

"God, thank You for reminding me that You
deeply care about me." (11/06)

"God, please guide me to grow in wisdom." (11/07)

"God, please remind me to stay rooted in Your Word as I
make decisions." (11/08)

"God, thank You for the reminders that I don't have to fear failure." (11/10)

"God, I want to turn from busyness toward You." (11/11)

"God, please remind me that You are Lord of my life." (11/12)

"God, please help me give my best to what I am currently
committed to." (11/14)

"God, my prayer is that I would surrender everything you have given
me back to You." (11/16)

"God, would You help me remember that it is impossible to
please everyone." (11/18)

"God, I pray for the ability to focus and be present." (11/21)

"God, help me cling to Your truth because Your truth is exactly what
makes us grow." (11/23)

"God, guide me to do the next best thing that is in front of me." (11/25)

I prayed the following prayer on November 27th and since then, I have seen God begin to transform my heart and change my perspective: *"Please help me turn around so that I can live a life that is slower and more purposeful rather than faster and less significant. I pray for Your help as I reorganize my activities and priorities. I pray for the ability to regroup and press on in a different way on a new path. God, I thank You for opening my eyes allowing me to see that I have been too busy. God, I don't know where I would have ended up, but I sure am thankful that You allowed me to realize what needs to change…"*

The reason I am writing this book is because I am currently journeying through what it means to abide and bear fruit. I knew God was calling me away from my state of being abundantly overwhelmed toward a life of fruitfulness. I would love for you to join me as I share what God has been teaching me. It is a privilege to grow alongside you as we discover God's plan to bear fruit in our lives together. I can't promise that this journey will be easy, but God's promise to us is that He can equip us to bear godly fruit. If a fruitful and abundant life sounds like something you need, join me as we discover what it means to abide in God's presence.

CHAPTER 1
Overwhelmingly Abundant

THE FATHER IS OUR GARDENER

"I am the true vine, and my Father is the gardener. He cuts off every branch in me that bears no fruit, while every branch that does bear fruit he prunes so that it will be even more fruitful. You are already clean because of the word I have spoken to you. Remain in me, as I also remain in you. No branch can bear fruit by itself; it must remain in the vine. Neither can you bear fruit unless you remain in me."
— John 15:1-4 (NIV)

There is no better way to begin our journey together than by discussing the blessing of God the Father as our Gardener. John 15 is one of the most beautiful passages in all of Scripture because it discusses our need for a Father who cares about the well-being of our hearts. The Father is immensely gracious to watch over us and provide for our needs. It is very humbling to recognize that He knows our true needs before we ask Him (Matthew 6:8). Because God knows the state and desires of our hearts, He has the ability to prune and cut the branches in our lives. As you read this chapter, I'd like you to picture a flourishing garden with growing fruits and vegetables. If we picture our hearts as a garden—abounding with potential to grow and flourish—we must recognize that there are hindrances to growth at times. For example, God as our Gardener has the power to cut off branches that need to be removed. As with a normal garden, some plants have branches that wither and die. Any well-experienced gardener would know that these are the branches that need to be removed so that new growth can emerge.

The Father as our Gardener has wisdom to see what needs to be cut away. Many things may need to be removed in order for us to grow properly. Sin is the root cause of dying branches. When seeds of sin are planted, we can never expect to see godly fruitfulness. Sin is the root of all evil. When these seeds of temptation are planted and sin enters our hearts, God is able to recognize diseased growth and cut off harmful branches. It is also helpful to remember that a sinful thought, word, or deed never only affects one person, place, or thing. Instead, its effects trickle to every big and small piece of our lives. We must be aware that God has the power to remove dead branches so that new life can grow. The process of cutting away is painful, but it is crucial if we desire to flourish in God's ways. When God prunes and cuts branches in our lives, He is not doing so in efforts to harm us. Instead, the opposite is true—God as our Gardener desires us to grow in healthy ways; therefore, He removes what is bad and fosters growth toward what is good. God the Father desires to give His people every good thing; therefore, His plans are not to harm us, but as Jeremiah 29:11 says, His plans are to provide us with hope and a bright future. Our lives are filled with godly fruit when we begin to trust God as our Gardener.

JESUS IS THE VINE AND WE ARE THE BRANCHES

"I am the vine; you are the branches. If you remain in me and I in you, you will bear much fruit; apart from me you can do nothing. If you do not remain in me, you are like a branch that is thrown away and withers; such branches are picked up, thrown into the fire and burned. If you remain in me and my words remain in you, ask whatever you wish, and it will be done for you. This is to my Father's glory, that you bear much fruit, showing yourselves to be my disciples."
— John 15:5-8 (NIV)

To understand the fruit-bearing process, we need to remember that Jesus is the Vine. In John 15, Jesus directly says that He is the Vine and we are the branches. In these verses, Jesus gives Himself and others distinct roles and describes how these roles should be fulfilled. Jesus says that if we want to be people that bear fruit, we need to remain in Him. "Remain" in this text describes the act of abiding. Understanding that we must remain in the Vine is crucial to grow fruit in our lives because without connection to the Vine, we are nothing. Jesus says that branches detached from Him wither and die. These branches are useless. In John 15, Jesus states that these branches are burned because they have separated and detached from the Vine. However, Jesus also says that those who remain connected to the Vine are able to ask for whatever they wish and it will be done.

Many people misunderstand this verse because it is often interpreted out of context. Take a moment and think about something you would wish for if you had the opportunity. We all have wishes that we hope to see granted one day. The question is not if we wish. Instead, the question we need to consider is "What are we wishing for?" Jesus desires our wish to align with His Word's teaching and His Kingdom's needs. For instance, John 15:7 does not imply that if I asked God for a new car, a new house, or a new pair of shoes, He would give them to me. This verse does not refer to asking and receiving in a worldly way. Instead, Jesus reminds us of His character in John 15:7. If we abide in Jesus, we have the freedom to ask Jesus to change our hearts and grow our minds. He has the power to transform our lives. Abiding in Jesus and asking Him for what we wish is a process designed to sanctify us. Jesus's biggest desire is to be with you and help you become more like Him. By asking God to grow the fruit of the Spirit and the qualities of Christ in our lives, we are able to receive blessings we can't even imagine. The fruit God desires to produce in our lives is much greater than anything the world could offer. For example, an amazing new car does not even begin to compare with the fruit God wants to produce in your life. In order to see and experience fruitfulness, we must remember that fruit comes from the Vine. This connection is vital because remaining attached to the Vine is how we experience spiritual life the way God intended. Jesus provides us with everything we need and allows us to bear fruit, but in order to experience this, we must establish an ongoing connection with Jesus. Our job is to stay connected to the Vine so the Holy Spirit can produce healthy, God-honoring fruit in and through us.

BEARING FRUIT THROUGH THE HOLY SPIRIT'S POWER

"But the fruit of the Spirit is love, joy, peace, patience, kindness, goodness, faithfulness, gentleness, self-control; against such things, there is no law." — Galatians 5:22-23 (ESV)

In John 15, God makes clear the call of each disciple of Jesus. To be a disciple of Christ and learn from Him, we must be willing to bear godly fruit. The central message of John 15 could be summarized in one simple phrase: "bear fruit." So far, we have learned that in order to bear fruit, we must acknowledge the Father as our Gardner and remain connected to Jesus, the Vine. Now, we are ready to discuss the calling of every Jesus follower—to bear fruit. We are going to explore the idea of bearing fruit together so that we can discover how God designed us to live. To understand the call to bear fruit, first we need to understand the meaning of fruit in the context of Galatians 5.

When God calls us to bear fruit, He is not telling us to collect apples and oranges in a basket. Instead, God is referring to spiritual fruit. In Galatians 5:22-23, Paul lists the fruit of the Spirit as love, joy, peace, patience, kindness, goodness, faithfulness, gentleness, and self control. These are the qualities that disciples of Jesus demonstrate as they walk with Him and learn His ways. Bruce Wilkinson wrote a book about bearing fruit called *Secrets of the Vine*. In his book, he outlines the impact of fruit on a person's life when he says, "Fruit is symbolized as the best result or sweetest prize in life."[2] Fruit is something valued by God; therefore, we should value fruit in our daily lives, too. If it matters to God, it should matter to us. Furthermore, Wilkinson says, "Fruit represents good works—a thought, attitude, or action of ours that God values because it glorifies Him." This explains how fruitfulness stems from our words, thoughts, attitudes, and actions. What we do, say, and think matters. These are the parts of our lives that have potential to bear godly fruit. We need to be careful about the ways we choose to behave because our mannerisms and habits can be used by God. Notice how I mentioned we choose to behave in certain ways. Behavior is a choice we make every single day. Let's allow our behavior to reflect the heart of Christ by committing to bearing godly fruit. In her book *Chasing Vines*, Beth Moore states, "Your fruit will outlast your life. You can't always see the effects because they are eternal, but one day you will see that you couldn't have been more significant if you tried."³ She discusses the significance of a fruitful life. It is powerful to recognize that the fruit God produces in and through us will last longer than our lives. Our fruit will outlive us; that's a hard concept to wrap our heads around, but it's important that we remember this truth. Moore mentions that fruit is long-lasting and can impact others in ways we do not yet know or see. She also talks about how being mindful of our behavior is crucial to living a life that bears God-honoring fruit. She asks a really powerful question for her readers that I would like us to consider as well: "Is what I'm doing (this action, approach, example, or instruction) bearing good fruit?" Asking yourself this question could help you determine what behaviors in your life are bearing godly fruit and which ones are not. I would encourage you to evaluate your behaviors (actions, thoughts, attitudes, approaches, examples, or instructions) with this question. Is your life bearing good fruit?

After evaluating the good fruit in our lives, we also must realize that bad fruit exists in our lives, too. God desires us to bear fruit, but this is limited to a certain kind of fruit. Godly fruit honors God and gives us the ability to grow into His likeness. However, because we are sinful, no one is capable of producing only good fruit. Jesus is the only one who is truly righteous. He is holy, blameless, and pure. Because of these qualities, Jesus always bears good fruit. We are not wired the same way because sin has stained our hearts. Even though we are incapable of producing good fruit perfectly like Jesus, He desperately desires that we abide in Him so He can produce good fruit in and through us. Moore says that the only part of fruit bearing that is worse than not bearing any fruit is bearing bad fruit. Jesus highly dislikes bad fruit and desires to equip us to produce good fruit. We must decide what we abide in because where we remain determines the direction of fruitfulness in our lives. Thankfully, God uses the sins and mistakes in our lives to cultivate growth. Even bad fruit is used by God to cultivate growth in our lives. God uses all things, our sins and our sanctification, to help us grow. In the garden of our hearts, God is able to use His shears of discipline and love to guide His people toward growth.

Hebrews 12:7-11 (NIV) says,

"Endure hardship as discipline; God is treating you as his children. For what children are not disciplined by their father? If you are not disciplined—and everyone undergoes discipline—then you are not legitimate, not true sons and daughters at all. Moreover, we have all had human fathers who disciplined us and we respected them for it. How much more should we submit to the Father of spirits and live! They disciplined us for a little while as they thought best; but God disciplines us for our good, in order that we may share in his holiness. No discipline seems pleasant at the time, but painful. Later on, however, it produces a harvest of righteousness and peace for those who have been trained by it."

These verses in Hebrews encourage us that God loves His children through the act of discipline. Discipline is difficult, but in order to grow as a disciple of Jesus, we must listen and receive the commands of Christ. Usually the process of pruning is not easy because it involves removing old branches of a plant so that new branches can grow. When healthy branches are cut, there is opportunity for healthy and strong growth. John 15:2 says that God cuts off every branch in us that bears no fruit, while every branch that does bear fruit he prunes so that it will be even more fruitful. It always seemed odd to me that God would cut branches bearing fruit. However, by reading and studying John 15, I have learned that God purposefully cuts prosperous parts of the plant, so that they can bear even more fruit as they are cultivated. God shears the branches of our hearts mindfully. He doesn't prune to inflict pain or cause distress. Instead, He prunes to reveal more opportunity for fruit to grow.

THE PRACTICE OF ABIDING

We have already discussed how crucial the act of abiding is to fruit-bearing; however, I want us to dive deeper into the practice of abiding. Understanding how to abide in Christ will guide us to live in the calling God has given us while bearing godly fruit. I love the way Wilkinson states the act of abiding. He says, "Abiding is all about the most important friendship of your life. Abiding doesn't measure how much you know about your faith or your Bible. In abiding, you seek, long for, thirst for, wait for, see, know, love, and hear, and respond to a person. More abiding means more of God in your life, more of Him in your activities, thoughts, and desires."[4] Many people make the mistake of thinking that fruit-bearing is about production. However, here we see that abiding is more about developing a friendship with God. If we place too much emphasis on production, our focus will shift from Jesus to ourselves. We are unable to produce fruit unless we abide in Jesus.

Therefore, we need to remind ourselves of what Jesus can do rather than focus on our own abilities.

Jesus can do far more than we ever ask, think, or imagine. Ephesians 3:20 (NIV) says, "Now to him who is able to do immeasurably more than all we ask or imagine, according to his power that is at work within us." Through His power, we become who we could not become on our own. The kind of transformation in John 15 only happens if we are willing to abide in Jesus. There is also immense value in resting in God's power. He is stronger, wiser, and more capable than we could ever be. The act of abiding can also be described as a recognition of humility. It takes a humble heart to accept the character of Christ and our human limitations. It is difficult surrendering pride and allowing God to work in the garden of our hearts. Committing our ways to the Lord is not an easy step to take. However, in humility, surrender, and commitment, we are able to rest in God's mighty hands and witness His great power. God does not want us to do more for Him. Instead, God wants us to be with Him more. If we are not focusing on abiding as the privilege to be with God, we are missing out on many blessings God has in store for us. Abiding is not the act of producing from our own strength as many may think. In fact, it is the opposite. Abiding is the act of resting in God, allowing Him to transform our hearts and produce the fruit of the Spirit to shine through us.

COLLEGE IS BANANAS!

During my first semester of college at Anderson University, I saw a friend of mine as I was walking to class. We had recently met one another and we waved to each other as we walked. As I approached him, I realized he was pretending to use a banana in his hand as a phone. Once he was done with his pretend phone call, he passed the banana to me. As I stood there with my friend's banana in my hand, I caught on to the banana phone call game and hesitantly decided to play along. After I had my fake conversation with his banana phone, I tried to give the banana back to my friend. However, he insisted on me keeping the banana even though I offered to give it back numerous times. I like bananas, but I did not prefer to eat a banana that he and I just pretended to use as a phone. Nevertheless, I ended up with the banana and we parted ways to arrive to class on time. As I walked, I wasn't sure what was more strange—the fact that he used the banana as a phone or the fact that he basically forced me to keep the banana. I arrived to class with the banana still in my hand and began thinking about this odd experience.

This strange story allowed me to realize something new about fruit. Unlike most other foods, fruits are quick to go bad. For example, bananas stay fresh for only 5-7 days. I don't know why my friend insisted that I kept his banana, but this helped me realize that fruit needs to be eaten before it goes bad. Most people enjoy fruits because of their unique textures, colors, shapes, and flavors. However, to enjoy fruit in these ways, you need to eat it while it is ripe and fresh. It is so sad to see good fruit go to waste because it was not eaten quickly enough. I believe God holds this perspective when He speaks to us in Galatians 5 about the fruit of the Spirit. Although the fruit of the Spirit are not actual fruit, they resemble the qualities of fruit almost exactly. Like the fruit that we eat, the fruit of the Spirit are all different. Also, each of the fruit of the Spirit requires a special environment to grow, healthy nutrients, and proper cultivation. Regardless of whether we are talking about spiritual fruit or edible fruit, both are best when freshly produced. Galatians 5:22-23 (ESV) says, "But the fruit of the Spirit is love, joy, peace, patience, kindness, goodness, faithfulness, gentleness, self-control; against such things, there is no law." Reading verse 23 reminds us that there is no law against the fruit of Spirit. In other words, God is asking us the question, "What are you waiting for?" I believe God desires to cultivate fruit in our lives and we are called to share it before it goes to waste. Therefore, we need to be aware of the calling God gives to each of us to bear fruit and share it with others.

FRUIT IN THE BIBLE

Fruit is a theme in the Bible that begins in Genesis and makes appearances throughout Scripture. Genesis 1:11-12 (NLT) says, "And God said, 'Let the earth sprout vegetation, plants yielding seed, and fruit trees bearing fruit in which is their seed, each according to its kind, on the earth.' And it was so. The earth brought forth vegetation, plants yielding seed according to their own kinds, and trees bearing fruit in which is their seed, each according to its kind. And God saw that it was good." God created plants to yield seed and designed fruit to grow as a part of His beautiful creation. Fruit is good for us to grow and consume. It is clearly a part of God's creational design. God delights in giving us fruit to eat that is healthy for us. For example, Psalm 104:14 (ESV) says, "You cause the grass to grow for the livestock and plants for man to cultivate, that he may bring forth food from the earth." God uses fruit to sustain His creation. Additionally, God commanded Adam and Eve to be fruitful in Genesis 1:28 (ESV): "God blessed them and said to them, 'Be fruitful and increase in number; fill the earth and subdue it. Rule over the fish in the sea and the birds in the sky and over every living creature that moves on the ground.'" God shows His desires for humans to be fruitful as they inherit the earth and dwell among His creation. Being fruitful is God's command ever since the beginning of human creation and this theme is spread throughout the entire Bible.

When we think of fruit, oftentimes we think of positive words like growth and abundance. However, in Genesis 3, we see that not all fruit is good for us. We need to be careful as to what fruit we cultivate and consume in our lives. In Genesis 3:6-7 (NIV), Adam and Eve eat fruit that they were not supposed to eat because God deemed it as unhealthy: "When the woman saw that the fruit of the tree was good for food and pleasing to the eye, and also desirable for gaining wisdom, she took some and ate it. She also gave some to Adam, who was with her, and he ate it. Then the eyes of both of them were opened, and they realized they were naked; so they sewed fig leaves together and made coverings for themselves." God created the tree of Knowledge of Good and Evil and told Adam and Eve not to eat the fruit of this tree. Genesis 2:8-9 (NIV) says, "Now the Lord God had planted a garden in the east, in Eden; and there he put the man he had formed. The Lord God made all kinds of trees grow out of the ground—trees that were pleasing to the eye and good for food. In the middle of the garden were the tree of life and the tree of the Knowledge of Good and Evil." Additionally, God informed them not to eat of the tree of Knowledge of Good and Evil as He commanded them in Genesis 2:15-17 (NIV): "The Lord God took the man and put him in the Garden of Eden to work it and take care of it. And the Lord God commanded the man, 'You are free to eat from any tree in the garden; but you must not eat from the tree of the Knowledge of Good and Evil, for when you eat from it you will certainly die.'" However, Eve was initially enticed by the serpent in the Garden of Eden and ate the fruit because he persuaded her that God's words were not true. Then, Eve convinced Adam to try the fruit. As a result of tasting the fruit, their eyes were opened, which means that sin entered the world and life would become much harder for Adam and Eve and their offspring. I find it interesting that as soon as Adam and Eve realized they were naked, they used another plant—fig leaves—to cover themselves. Adam and Eve felt shame for disobeying God. In response to Adam and Eve's disobedience, God made men work the ground and gave women pain during childbirth. Both men and women's responsibilities became more difficult after Adam and Eve sinned against God. Because Adam and Eve ate the fruit God commanded them not to eat, God's people continue to struggle in sin. Therefore, we are called to be careful because the fruit we consume determines the fruit we produce. God clearly intends some fruit for our good, as He placed many trees and plants in the Garden of Eden for Adam and Eve's enjoyment. However, trees like the Knowledge of Good and Evil are ones that are dangerous for us. We need to ensure that we are desiring and producing the healthy fruits God designed for us and not the harmful ones.

The theme from Genesis with the tree of Knowledge of Good and Evil returns in the last chapter of the book of Revelation. Revelation 22:1-2 (ESV) says, "The angel showed me the river of the water of life, bright as crystal, flowing from the throne of God and of the Lamb through the middle of the street of the city; also, on either side of the river, the tree of life with its twelve kinds of fruit, yielding its fruit each month. The leaves of the tree were for the healing of the nations." This text highlights lively creation just like Genesis 1. The tree of life is mentioned in Genesis, but it is referred to in Revelation as a tree with twelve kinds of fruit yielding its fruit each month. This describes the new heavens and new earth. Although we are unsure exactly what that will look like, Scripture points to the fact that plants and trees are involved as well as the fruit they produce. It is interesting to know that the Bible both begins and ends with an account of fruit. This is God's way of informing us that our lives should be fruitful from beginning to end. God specifies how to live a fruitful life through the pages of Scripture. However, Galatians 5 is a well-known passage because it specifically describes the fruit of the Spirit. These qualities summarize what a fruitful life as a Christian should look like. Love, joy, peace, patience, kindness, goodness, faithfulness, gentleness, and self control are the fruit of the Spirit. Pursuing these attributes are foundational for God's people.

THE FORMATION OF FRUIT

Did you know that fruit is created through the growth of a flower? The flower's inner parts contain seeds that are dispersed by humans, animals, and nature. When these seeds are planted in fertile ground, they are able to produce healthy and abundant fruit. Similarly, as we grow as believers, God describes our growth as that of a plant. First, it is important to recognize that God is the one that allows all things to grow. 1 Corinthians 3:7 (NIV) says, "So neither he who plants nor he who waters is anything, but only God who gives the growth." This refers to physical things that grow, like plants and flowers. However, it also refers to the growth we experience spiritually in our hearts. God desires healthy fruit to fill our lives so that we may live purposefully. Psalm 103:15-16 (NIV) says, "The life of mortals is like grass, they flourish like a flower of the field; the wind blows over it and it is gone, and its place remembers it no more." In these verses, our lives are referred to as ones that flourish like flowers. Our lives fade quicker than we would like to realize. Therefore, we need to remember to live fruitful lives to honor the Lord with the time He gives us by honoring Him with our first fruits. Proverbs 3:9 (ESV) says, "Honor the Lord with your wealth and with the first fruits of all your produce." Producing fruit for the Lord is necessary as we live our lives for His glory. This is the way we make the most of our lives on earth. Another reminder comes from Isaiah 40:8 (ESV): "The grass withers, the flower fades, but the word of our God will stand forever." Remembering that we wither away, but God and His truth last forever is crucial to living a fruitful life. God's Word is the source of all beneficial aspects of life on earth; therefore, we should hold tightly to the truth. God's Word is greater than we are and lasts longer than we will, so we should submit our lives to God and let His Word dictate our path rather than the world.

There is no law against love, joy, peace, patience, kindness, goodness, faithfulness, gentleness, or self-control. Keeping in step with the Spirit offers freedom from the law and commitment to the Lord. Paul writes that people do not need to be conceited, provoking one another or envying each other. Instead, God's people are called to crucify the flesh along with its worldly desires. Jesus reminds His people of His death on the cross through Paul's writing. As Jesus's followers, Christians are called to take up their crosses and follow Him. Jesus does not say that this process will be easy; however, the flesh must be dealt with because in Jesus, people can live above the desires and passions of the flesh. Living life in Jesus is greater than anything of the flesh because Jesus is superior to anything in heaven and on earth and equips His people with the Holy Spirit to live a life of freedom in Christ. We are able to experience abundant blessing through the Spirit's work in and through us. As the Spirit nourishes us, we are able to grow in the fruit of the Spirit. Ask the Holy Spirit to make you aware of the work He is performing in your heart and mind. Be intentional as God reveals Himself to you through His people, His power, and His presence. Also, be attentive as God teaches you more about Himself through the nine fruits of the Spirit, because He will use them to change your life!

HOW TO BEST UTILIZE THIS STUDY:

As you walk through this study, I want to make sure you read through this as slowly or as quickly as you need. Take time to learn about the fruit of the Spirit as well as other Christ-like qualities highlighted throughout Scripture. Outside of the nine fruits of the Spirit, there are other fruits that are produced as results of the fruit of the Spirit at work in a person's life. In this book, I have paired each of the fruit of the Spirit with a subsequent characteristic:

> Love creates unity amongst God's people.
>
> Joy yields strength in everyday activities for God's people.
>
> Peace allows God's people to surrender everything to Him.
>
> Patience fosters intentionality in God's people as they wait on Him and conquer challenges.
>
> Kindness cultivates generosity within the people of God as they recognize what He has done for them.
>
> Goodness provides perseverance in difficulty within God's people.
>
> Faithfulness equips God's people to trust Him deeply in all circumstances.
>
> Gentleness coincides with the development of humility in the hearts of God's people.
>
> Lastly, self-control empowers God's people with the freedom they need to live a God-honoring life.

The fruit of the Spirit serve as a wonderful foundation of qualities the Spirit produces; however, the fruit of the Spirit are simply the beginning of God's transformative process in our hearts. I have provided supplemental questions for reflection as well as Scripture passages and other helpful resources to deepen your understanding of the fruit of the Spirit. I have written prayers in response to each lesson, but please write your own prayers as well to extend your study time. I have also shared a few worship songs that have reminded me of each fruit of the Spirit. If worship songs help you process the Word of God, please listen to the songs suggested. The goal throughout this study is to truly understand each fruit of the Spirit and learn to cultivate them in our daily walk of faith. As we begin our journey together, please utilize all resources within this study at your own pace as you follow along in each section. I am excited to walk with you as we learn more about the fruit of the Spirit together!

CHAPTER 2
Love

Don't you think our world needs more love? Our world craves the real love of God. The world has a variety of expressions of love, but what we need most is the biblical way of love taught in Scripture. For example, I can say that I love dark chocolate. I can also say that I love my family and friends. Most importantly, I love the Lord. My love for dark chocolate, family and friends, and the Lord are all distinctly different. Love can be used in multiple ways throughout the English language. For example, my love for dark chocolate is ever so small in comparison to my love for the Lord. However, God's meaning of love is much deeper than the world's definition of love. God's love describes a commitment rather than simply a feeling. It is more than an emotion because love in the Christian life describes how to live. The word "love" in Greek is, *agape*. This kind of love includes more than just happy and affectionate feelings. Instead, it represents a deep level of relational commitment. The word "love" in Hebrew is *ahavah*, and it suggests a similar meaning as the Greek definition.

Love is not earned by good works, but love is spread by good works. God is love and He gave us the command to love Him and others. In fact, God gave us this guidance as the greatest commandment in Scripture. Of all the commandments God desires us to remember, He emphasizes one: to love others. It amazes me that there are 613 commandments in the Old Testament law that God gave to the Israelites. In Matthew 22, Jesus interacts with a Pharisee. In this conversation, Jesus summarizes all 613 commandments in four verses of Scripture. He was asked by a Pharisee, "Teacher, which is the greatest commandment in the Law?" (verse 36). Jesus replied, "Love the Lord your God with all your heart and with all your soul and with all your mind. This is the first and greatest commandment" (verses 37-38). Jesus summarized all the commandments of the Old Testament by telling the Pharisee to love God the Father completely. The second greatest commandment is loving your neighbor as yourself (verse 39). The last verse of this passage states that all the Law and Prophets hang on these two commandments (verse 40). When Matthew referenced "all the Law and Prophets," he was referring to Old Testament Scriptures. God desires that we love Him and love others. Let's take a deeper look at what it looks like to love as God commands in His Word.

As we explore the quality of love, please read these verses below carefully:

"Love is patient and kind; love does not envy or boast; it is not arrogant or rude. It does not insist on its own way; it is not irritable or resentful; it does not rejoice at wrongdoing, but rejoices with the truth. Love bears all things, believes all things, hopes all things, endures all things. Love never ends. As for prophecies, they will pass away; as for tongues, they will cease; as for knowledge, it will pass away."
— 1 Corinthians 13:4-8 (ESV)

"And above all these put on love, which binds everything together in perfect harmony." — Colossians 3:14 (ESV)

"Greater love has no one than this, that someone lay down his life for his friends." — John 15:13 (ESV)

What do the verses above communicate about love?

2021 SENIOR PRANK

Most high school seniors are given the exciting option of planning a senior prank. In 2021, it was finally time for me and my classmates to participate in this fun tradition. At the end of the school year, my class brainstormed ideas to prank our school. Some students suggested we bring our pets to school, while others liked the idea of putting mac and cheese in the bathroom sinks throughout the high school building. Because there were so many differing opinions, we decided to collaborate and combine a few ideas into one big prank. We decided we were going to "fork" the outside of our high school building and place plastic cups filled halfway with water on the inside of the building about 6 inches apart from one another on the floor. Then, to take our prank to the next level, we decided to camp outside of the school building that night. The school approved our crazy ideas, and they agreed to our senior prank plan.

Before I left my house to participate in our senior prank, my family helped me prepare for the night. My dad and my brothers love to go camping, so they equipped me with everything I needed for camping outside the school building. I brought a sleeping bag, a tent, a pillow, and a large flashlight. Some other students brought the rest of the supplies required for "cupping" the hallways and "forking" the landscaping. Thankfully, our guidance counselor kindly agreed to admit my senior class into the high school building at night. Quickly, my senior class assembled and distributed tasks to everyone. My guidance counselor watched with amazement as we started by filling the entire downstairs of our building and the stairways with plastic cups containing water. We also included a large "Senior Class of 2021" plastic cup design in the middle of our lunchroom to add some fun flair to our prank. After two long hours, we finished lining the hallways with red and white plastic Solo cups. Each cup was filled with water, so we had to tiptoe around the cups to prevent them from falling over and spilling. We tried our best to be careful yet efficient as we filled cups with water and placed them all over the floor. Then, we transitioned outside of the building and placed forks in the ground around the school landscaping. After the landscaping around the school was decorated with plastic forks, we began helping one another set up our tents. This process was hilarious because you could easily tell those of us who had been camping before and those of us who had never been camping based on how long it took to set up our tents. Some people had their tents ready in seconds, whereas other people took thirty minutes to set up their tents. It was also interesting to see inside our tents. As I looked around, I saw a few plain tents with a sleeping bag or two inside and I saw others with stringed lights, comfy mattresses, and duffle bags of clothing. Although the goal was to sleep outside in our tents, the tents probably weren't necessary because none of us slept at all.

After setting up our tents, we stayed awake by playing a game called Secret Hitler. As we played Secret Hitler, a police officer arrived in front of the high school. When everyone noticed the police, the shouts and laughs died down instantly. We were concerned as the officer walked toward us; however, he approached us with a warm smile and simply stated that he saw our group having fun and wanted to join! The police officer talked with us for about thirty minutes, and we took a selfie with him. He explained to us that on night shifts, he stays in his car for most of the time unless there is an issue that arises, so he appreciated the fact that we were able to entertain him. After the policeman left and we finished our most recent round of Secret Hitler, we finally decided to wind down at 4:00 A.M. Whether we fell asleep or not, most of us were awake at about 5:45 A.M. because a few teachers arrived at school extremely early to take down our prank. Teachers began taking away every cup laid on the floor before any other students could see our masterpiece. It had taken hours to fill each cup with water and spread them around our school, so my class was very disappointed when we were awakened so early by the teachers destroying our hard work. The plastic cups filled with water throughout the school blocked students from moving in the hallways which was kind of the point of the prank, but that would be very problematic to the flow of a normal school day. Although I was tired the next day after receiving almost no sleep, our senior prank was a very exciting experience for me. Although the majority of our cups were removed before students and other faculty arrived at school that morning, our senior prank provided immense unity. That night was one of the best experiences for the CDS class of 2021; however our class hasn't always navigated conflict well.

DIFFERENCES LED TO DIVISION

There are many students at my school who have been considered "lifers" because they have attended since kindergarten; however, I was new to the CDS class of 2021 during my freshman year of high school. One of the very first things I noticed was the widespread differences in talents, personalities, and interests. I have attended many different schools because my family has moved frequently, but I have never encountered a group like the CDS class of 2021. I discovered that there were many similarities I shared among people and there were many differences, too. I loved it!

Unfortunately, the differences amongst the class (more often than not) led to separation rather than unity. Cliques formed, which automatically created boundaries amongst me and my peers. Seeing the separate groups form during my freshman year was disheartening; however, I was hopeful because I believed that as our grade matured and as the Lord worked in our hearts, we could embrace our differences. As freshmen, sophomores, and even juniors, my class generally let our differences create feelings of fear and separation. This saddened my heart because I saw incredible amounts of potential in our class. However, I kept praying for unity amongst our grade because I knew all we needed was God's power and the consistent effort of working together.

LOVE WORKING THROUGH UNITY

During our high school years, my grade eventually chose not to stay in the comfort zone of our closest friends. We stopped letting fearful thoughts control our actions and we committed to unifying. When my class learned the value of our differences, the entire environment changed. Individuals who had been avoiding each other were able to work together. Students who needed help with math were able to confidently ask for help from classmates who excelled in math. Athletes who played in fall sports encouraged others who played in spring sports by coming to support them at their games and competitions. People who had dominant personalities began to talk less and listen more to those who needed an opportunity to speak so that those who were on the shy side were able to share their unique gifts.

I was able to witness these kinds of changes (and more) among the CDS class of 2021 my senior year. We committed to working together as the body of Christ. All parts of the body of Christ are given a different function, yet none of the parts work properly without the others assisting them. 1 Corinthians 12:12 (NIV) tells us that "Just as a body, though one, has many parts, but all its many parts form one body, so it is with Christ." This demonstration accurately describes the transition my CDS class of 2021 experienced. At first, we heavily depended on ourselves and those who acted like us, looked like us, or participated in similar activities. However, as senior year arrived, we realized we had developed the wrong perspective. We needed to depend on each other for the senior class body of students to function to its fullest potential. Do not wait to notice this perspective and change your point of view like my senior class did. It would have been amazing if my class would have recognized the benefit of loving others through unity earlier. However, this proves that unity requires a certain level of maturity and growth. Therefore, in your life, whether it be your school, home, gym, or workplace, ask God to help you understand ways to pursue unity. Through the body of Christ, you and others can begin growing more fully as members of God's family.

According to the dictionary definition, love is defined as great interest and pleasure in something. When my class developed interest and pleasure in one another, the atmosphere shifted. Our class hung out together and enjoyed one another, not because we were all the same, but because we were different. We all have the wonderful opportunity to rejoice in our unique qualities. The shift that occurred within my classmates my senior year might be one of the coolest changes I have ever witnessed because love inspired the change. Love for each other brings people beautifully together. God reminds us that He loved the whole world and sent His Son to die for everyone. Love is the essential part of our calling as individuals. Because God loves everyone, we are created to do the same. Matthew 22:36-40 describes the two greatest commandments as loving God and loving people. We are designed by Love Himself to be loved and to reciprocate His love to our neighbors. Love helps both us and others reach our full potential in Christ Jesus. My class would not have been able to decide on a senior prank or much less accomplish a senior prank if it weren't for the love God pours into us and the love we poured into each other. Even though my high school classmates and I aren't all together on a school campus anymore, God equipped us in high school to embrace differences and tap into the best kind of potential that exists—His everlasting love. Just as my senior class filled hundreds of plastic cups with water for our senior prank, fill up your cup with love and then pour it into others' lives so they can be unified with others and with Christ.

BIBLICAL LOVE AND UNITY

As I read the Bible, a theme that I enjoy recognizing is love because it is laced through every part of Scripture. For example, the Holy Trinity is a bond of love. The Father, Son, and Spirit are bound by love and unified as one God. Without the Father, the Son could not have died on the cross for everyone's sins. It is made very clear that Jesus came to complete the will of the Father (John 6:38, John 5:30, John 4:34, Luke 22:42). Jesus states very clearly in the Bible that His power to teach, heal, and perform miracles comes from the Father (John 5:19-20, John 8:54, Luke 10:22). Additionally, the Father's love for His people could not have been made complete without the Son. Sadly, sin separated God's people from Him. When people sinned and desired reconciliation with God in the Old Testament, priests were utilized to offer sacrifices to God so that God could forgive those in need of restoration. However, when the Son died as the ransom for all sins, we were given the freedom to ask for forgiveness through Jesus Christ. Now, God's people are able to live a new life hidden in Christ with God (Colossians 3:3). Jesus did not come to make "bad" people "good." Jesus came to make "dead" people "alive." Because Jesus saved us from sin and granted us a new life, we are considered new creations (2 Corinthians 5:17). Jesus served as the bridge to unite God's people to the Father. After Jesus rose from the dead, He ascended to heaven to reunite with the Father. Now, the Father and the Son rely on the Spirit. Jesus was no longer physically present with His people on earth, but the Spirit came not only to be with God's people, but to dwell inside of them (1 Corinthians 3:16). The Holy Spirit serves as our Helper (John 14:15-17, 26). The Spirit of the Lord gives us freedom (2 Corinthians 3:17). Through the Holy Spirit, we can withstand trials and temptations of many kinds. It is evident that each role of the Trinity is different; however, the Father, Son, and the Spirit are unified as God and held together by love.

> ...the Father, Son, and the Spirit are unified as God and held together by love.

The Trinity is a wonderful example of love because the Father, Son, and Spirit are the same God; however, they each have a different role. This parallels our identity as Christians because each of God's people have different roles within the Kingdom of God, but all are children of God who belong to Him and receive identity from Him. Love is what holds the Trinity together; therefore, the Trinity is not possible without love. If the Trinity requires love, then we as God's people definitely need love in our relationships, too. We are the body of Christ; therefore, love is an irreplaceable addition to cultivating God's family. Because the Trinity provides abundant love for God's people, let's decide to accept the love of God with gratitude. We need to be people that seek to grow stronger, unifying bonds with people and with God because that is exactly what Jesus did while He was on earth. Jesus sought His Father in all things and remained devoted to Him while also making disciples from all nations (1 John 3:16). Let's do what Jesus did by embracing the call to love God and love people.

In God's Word, the body of Christ is often referred to as "brothers and sisters." The body of Christ is described well in Ephesians 1:13 (NIV) which says, "And you also were included in Christ when you heard the message of truth, the gospel of your salvation. When you believed, you were marked in Him with a seal, the promised Holy Spirit." When my class realized that we are all brothers and sisters in Christ, our perspectives and experiences drastically changed. When we identified ourselves as brothers and sisters, we did not conform to a certain image, but instead, we remained who God called us to be and committed to love. God created every person "fearfully and wonderfully" (Psalm 139:14) and we are designed in His image (Genesis 1:26-27). The body of Christ is beautiful because it is composed of people who were created by God, but it also includes those who are different from one another. My senior class hesitated to fully love one another because we were diverse in interests, personalities, abilities, etc. Diversity seems to be a factor in people shying away from love; however, it is the perfect ingredient to enhance strength in the body of Christ. I have found that I get along with many people who are different from me because they have different strengths than I do. When I surround myself with people that are different from me, God always teaches me more about His character and overflows blessings in my relationships. I love that God's design for love includes diversity. God does not shy away from diversity in the body of Christ, but instead, He welcomes and encourages it because it is required for love to flourish. God blesses His people with a spiritual family because once we are cleansed by the blood of Christ, we are united with others who have also devoted their lives to the Lord. We are a people united for the sole purpose of loving God and loving people. Ephesians 4:5-6 (NIV) says, "There is one faith, one baptism, one God and Father who is over all and through all and in all." God's Word makes it very clear that He is to be the focus for the body of Christ. People from every "tribe, nation, and tongue" are called to use what God has given them to exalt His name (Revelation 5:9). Our goal is to witness more people coming to Christ by receiving the gift of salvation. God's role is transformation, and our role is communication. Let's be people to seek unity by sharing God's love and spreading the gospel.

PRAY

Dear Lord,

Thank You for allowing Your love to overflow in my life. Please use the love You graciously pour into me to show others who You are. Equip me to love people that are like me and those who are different from me. Help me pursue unity among my brothers and sisters. Surround me with Your love and remind me that loving You and loving others are the two greatest commandments You give to Your people. Allow love to flourish in my life so that I and others will reach the complete fullness of our God-given destinies. Amen

PRAISE

Song: "With One Voice" by Transformation Church Worship

PAUSE

1. Who is someone God is calling you to love who may be different from you?

2. What did you learn about love from the Trinity?

3. What are ways God could cultivate love and unity through you in your workplace, school, home, campus, etc.?

READ: EPHESIANS 4:1-16

1. What do these verses reveal about God?

2. What do these verses reveal about you?

3. What do you hear God calling you to do in response to reading these verses?

REMEMBER

The world pursues disunity among one another, but Jesus followers pursue unity in the body of Christ through the fruit of love.

CHAPTER 3
Joy

Have you ever met someone who is abundantly joyful? Maybe a friend, family member, co-worker, coach, mentor, or teacher comes to mind? One of the most joyful people I know is someone I met at the YMCA during my freshman year of college. Mrs. Donna, a sweet friend of mine, works at the front desk at my local YMCA. The first time I came to the YMCA and met Mrs. Donna, I could sense her joy immediately. When she introduced herself to me, she had a bright smile on her face, and I could sense God had given her the gift of joy. When I first interacted with Mrs. Donna, I knew she loved the Lord because Scripture flowed from her lips, and she spoke kindly with encouragement. I am so thankful that every time I visit the YMCA, I am able to see Mrs. Donna. She has taught me more about what true joy looks like because her joy has proven to withstand even difficult circumstances. As we talk together during the week at the YMCA, Mrs. Donna always gives glory to God and says that He is the source of her joy. I began to see Mrs. Donna throughout the week when I went to the YMCA and over time, we have gotten to know each other better. Our friendship over the last few years was one of the biggest blessings during my college journey! During my junior year of college, I did not see Mrs. Donna for a few days, which was odd because we almost always saw each other at least once or twice a week. I texted Mrs. Donna to see if she was okay and she told me that she had been at home because she fell and broke her knee. Thankfully, she was on the road to recovery almost immediately. Recovering from knee injuries is not easy and often takes time, patience, and diligence. However, Mrs. Donna handled this challenge with continual joy. Every time I asked her how her knee was doing, she always responded by saying that God was healing her knee and teaching her more about His character. Isn't that amazing? Mrs. Donna trusted God would heal her and leaned into Him as she faced this challenge. Even when she wasn't fully healed yet, Mrs. Donna chose to be joyful and depend on the faithfulness of God. I admire Mrs. Donna's demeanor and I desire to be as joyful as she is, too! Mrs. Donna has taught me that even in the most difficult seasons, God always gives us reasons to be joyful. God is with us and gives us the ability to choose joy. Mrs. Donna helped me understand that joy lasts beyond circumstances. It is a fruit from those who build their foundation on the Lord. The Greek word for joy is *chará*. Joy is described as cheer and gladness of heart from the Holy Spirit. In Hebrew, "joy" is the word *simchah*. This word is related to the idea of grace which expresses itself through gratitude to the Lord. The Greek and Hebrew definitions of the word "joy" remind us of the hope we have in the Lord and His promises. Joy is rooted deeper than circumstances because it is a foundational blessing in the Bible. The truth in God's Word is always relevant and applicable; therefore, joy is a gift always available to those who trust in Him.

As we explore joy, please read the verses below:

"May the God of hope fill you with all joy and peace in believing, so that by the power of the Holy Spirit you may abound in hope."
— Romans 15:13 (NIV)

"Rejoice in the Lord always; again, I will say, Rejoice."
— Philippians 4:4 (NIV)

"You make known to me the path of life; in your presence, there is fullness of joy; at your right hand are pleasures forevermore."
— Psalm 16:11 (ESV)

What do the verses above communicate about joy?

DANCING OR RUNNING?

Do you have any siblings? I enjoy having three amazing siblings—two brothers and one sister. Although my siblings drive me crazy sometimes, they are huge blessings in my life. I am grateful for the relationships I have with each of my siblings, but there is something extra special about having a sister. My sister and I are very different, but that does not hinder the fact that I love my sister, Mary Claire. Over our twenty years together as sisters, our relationship has been through many changes. We have journeyed through so many phases together, but one activity my sister and I consistently enjoyed was dance. I began dancing when I was three years old, and my sister began when she turned three, too. As our skills improved, we took dancing much more seriously. Dancing is very special to me because Mary Claire and I performed in recitals together and practiced our routines with each other. We have so many fun dance memories!

When I entered my eighth-grade year of middle school, I decided to run on my school's cross country team. I had never run before, but my friend's mom encouraged me to try out for the team to see if I would enjoy the sport. At first, I didn't enjoy running. I remember during our team tryouts I stopped to tie my shoes which was really just an excuse to catch my breath from being winded. I had never run on a consistent basis, so I was not up to par with the normal level of training for a runner because I had always been a dancer. Although it wasn't my favorite at first, I decided to continue running cross country at least a few more days after tryouts so I could learn about the sport, make friends on the team, know the coach better, and attend practices to see if I improved at all. After a few more days went by, I decided to try running for another week. Soon enough, one week turned into another and I began to really enjoy running as I continued to grow in my relationships with those on the team and improve my fitness abilities. To my surprise, I learned to love running. Eighth grade was a highlight of my middle school years because I was able to continue dancing and pursue my new love for running at the same time. However, once my family moved to Charlotte, North Carolina, the summer before my freshman year of high school, I knew I could not pursue both running and dancing because that would be too much to balance on top of school, extra-curricular activities, and relationships with friends and family. I had a tough decision to make because I felt God stirring in my heart a desire to run. I wanted to continue cross country and join track in high school; however, I knew that dancing was important too, especially because I danced with my sister.

Mary Claire and I tried intensive camps at several dance studios the summer we moved to Charlotte. As we visited different dance studios, I could sense the Lord telling me dance was not the calling He planned for me as I transitioned into high school. I was hesitant about continuing to dance; however, my sister confidently knew that she wanted to continue dancing. She wanted to dance competitively, but that was never a desire for me. Although it was a hard decision, I stopped my twelve-year dancing career to pursue my newfound love for running. I have no regrets in choosing to run because the Lord has both challenged me and blessed me immensely through this sport. However, because my sister and I were involved in different activities, we did not see each other as often. Thankfully, for the first three years my family lived in Charlotte, my sister and I attended the same school. I loved seeing my sister at school because typically, after school, we would be in different places. I would run with my team while she would dance with her team. However, before my senior year and my sister's sophomore year, Mary Claire decided to switch schools to pursue dance on a deeper level. She applied to a dance program at an art school and was accepted! While I was excited for her to enter a dance program at a new school, I was also discouraged because I knew we would see each other even less because we would constantly be in different places not only after school, but during school as well. For instance, Mary Claire's new school started later than my school, so I did not see her most mornings. Also, when I came back from cross country or track practices in the afternoon, Mary Claire had already left to attend her dance classes at night. It became harder to maintain a relationship with my sister because we ended up at different schools and pursued different and time-consuming activities after school.

Mary Claire and I are very different from one another, so the fact that we attended different schools and participated in different activities didn't surprise me. I was grateful that she was able to enhance her love for dancing while I was able to pursue my love for running. I am glad God led us to enjoy the different passions He placed in our hearts. It was difficult at first, but I am thankful He closed the door for dancing and opened the door for running in my life. When I entered eighth grade, I noticed my love for dance had faded. The reason why my love for dancing diminished was not that I wanted to quit, but because I discovered a greater love for running. I was really excited to run on the cross country and track teams at my new high school, but I was still disappointed that Mary Claire and I were not together very often. Sometimes, even though we lived in the same house, I wouldn't see Mary Claire the entire day. I knew I had to do something to bridge the gap between our busy, opposite schedules.

CUTETITOS AND CHICK-FIL-A

Thankfully, my sister and I found a solution to our opposite schedules. We decided to meet Monday nights for dinner and a Target run. My practices ended early enough on Mondays to meet, and Mary Claire did not dance until later in the evenings on Mondays, so this time frame worked well for both of us. First, we would eat dinner at Chick-Fil-A and then we would visit Target right across the street. When my sister and I visited Target, we looked for one specific item on the shelf in the toy aisle. Our item of purchase every Monday night at Target was a toy called a Cutetito. After the first couple of weeks, we started an official collection of these stuffed animal toys. One Monday evening Mary Claire would pick out a Cutetito and the next Monday, I would choose one. We took turns picking out Cutetitos each week. As a result, we each have at least twenty because this fun tradition occurred most of my senior year and her sophomore year. Although these toys are quite hilarious, the real reason we purchased these stuffed animals was to create memories together.

This amazing tradition my sister and I share began when my family went out to eat one night. After dinner and dessert, my mom shared a great idea: "How about we go into Target and pick out the strangest item we can find? We will each have ten minutes to look!" We all agreed, so our destination before we returned home was Target. My family did a great job with this challenge, and we collected some weird items. I distinctly remember walking down the toy aisle when I discovered Cutetitos which are stuffed animals that come wrapped in a blanket. Who wouldn't be intrigued by a Cutetito?! I brought the stuffed animal with me, and my family looked at me with wide-eyed expressions when I proudly displayed my discovery. Because my family was interested in seeing what the Cutetito looked like, my parents agreed to buy it. At home, I slowly unwrapped the stuffed animal from its blanket. The Cutetito series at Target was called the "Pizzaitos Series," so each stuffed animal came wrapped in a pizza blanket. The different types of Cutetitos in this specific series were all named after pizza toppings. For instance, our Cutetito was a ladybug named "Olivito." My sister and I immediately fell in love with my new Cutetito discovery. Ever since this fun family moment in Target, Mary Claire and I carried this joy into our lives each Monday evening. The reason Mary Claire and I went to dinner and looked in the Target toy aisles was not to simply eat at Chick-Fil-A and buy a fun toy. Although that made me smile, nothing makes me smile more than sharing moments of joy with my sister. Joy is one of the fruits of the Spirit that can be described as a feeling of great pleasure and happiness. The time my sister and I spent together (even though it only totaled to about an hour every Monday) brought me immense joy.

JOY IS A FORM OF STRENGTH

I have a confession to share with you about time with my sister each week. Sometimes, I would drive to meet my sister on Mondays and think, "Do I have time for this?" It was so easy for my thoughts to become consumed by the long to-do list in my head. I quickly realized I needed to stop asking myself this question because I was able to learn a valuable lesson through meeting with my sister: there is always time for joy—even small moments of joy – no matter how busy you are. Moments of joy serve as the strength that will allow us to conquer the busy parts of life. For example, after being with my sister, I found it much easier to find the motivation to complete items on my to-do list because joy was the fuel that powered me through. I remind myself that joy is always present, but sometimes, it takes intentionality to set apart time to recognize the joy God has showered in your life. To experience joy, do something you love! For example, being outside is something that brings me joy, so I often run or walk or complete parts of my to-do list outside. You may not be able to spend an entire day doing the things you enjoy, but start by carving out a small amount of time to devote toward a joyful activity. You will be surprised at how just a few minutes can transform your day to one filled with more joy.

> *Moments of joy serve as the strength that will allow us to conquer the busy parts of life.*

INTENTIONAL PAUSES

Something that has brought me joy recently is stopping throughout my day to take intentional pauses. I find that busyness can often take away my joy because when I am focused on my to-do list, too often I find myself overwhelmed. However, taking a moment to enjoy the environment around me brings me so much joy. When I am studying, I like to pause and pray that God would give me the strength to keep learning. When I am outside, I like to pause and pray by praising God for

His beautiful creation. When I am eating a meal, I like to pause and pray thanking God for the food He provided for me. Intentional pauses and prayer have helped me experience much more joy. Whether you are finishing math homework, working from home, or taking care of children, use small moments of time to pause and pray because you will feel more joy as you refresh your heart and mind. The very best way to experience joy is through interacting with Jesus because joy is who Jesus is! Psalm 16:11 (ESV) says, "In His presence, there is fullness of joy; at your right hand are pleasures forevermore." The joy of the Lord is contagious. Joy is found in His presence. I remind myself constantly that joy is from Jesus, and He will reveal joy in our hearts if we pause to be with Him. Take moments of intentional pauses to recognize and experience the joy of Jesus throughout your day.

GRATITUDE YIELDS JOY

My mom always says, "Grateful people are the happiest people." This is wonderful advice that I have found to be extremely important. As I mentioned earlier, the intentional pauses in my life allow me to stop and reflect on my surroundings. Even in the hardest of days or craziest of situations, there is always something to be thankful for. Romans 8:39 (NIV) says, "Neither height nor depth, nor anything else in all creation will ever be able to separate us from the love of God that is in Christ Jesus our Lord." If anything, we can be grateful that the Lord is always with us because nothing at all separates us from Him. Gratitude is the secret to being joyful because focusing on what God has given us re-centers our perspective from the things we lack to His abundant blessings. If you desire more joy in your life, ask God for a more grateful heart.

> *If you desire more joy in your life, ask God for a more grateful heart.*

We often try satisfying our need for joy with things that ultimately promote feelings of depression and anxiety. It seems as though our world prefers temporary solutions to experience joy. Fulfilling earthly values can bring people small amounts of joy, but the joy God offers is

> *Fulfilling earthly values can bring people small amounts of joy, but the joy God offers is eternal.*

eternal. So many people walk down destructive paths desperately searching for joy, but they fail to realize that they don't need to go on a search for joy. Instead, the joy of the Lord is everywhere because God is omnipresent and serves as the epitome of joy. The Lord tells Nehemiah in Scripture, "The joy of the Lord is your strength" (Nehemiah 8:10). The same joy that was available to Nehemiah is available to you and me. Choose to satisfy your heart with the only Person able to fill your true desires, Jesus Christ. Intentionally focusing on the Lord as the source of our joy will bring bountiful blessings in our lives.

PRAY

Dear Heavenly Father,
Please remind me that Your presence is joy's dwelling place. Reveal to me Your joy in the big and small areas of my life. God, help me take time to experience the vast joys of life even when I am going through hard circumstances. Remind me that joy isn't only a feeling, but it is a strength when we recognize its beauty and power. Lord, help me experience more joy in my life by spending time with You and participating in activities that honor You. Amen.

PRAISE

Song: "Joyful" by Dante Bowe

PAUSE

1. How can you implement moments of joy in your life (even if they are small)?

2. What are some areas you can pause to reflect on the joy of the Lord?

3. How can you spend more time in God's presence to experience strength from God's sustaining joy?

READ: 2 CORINTHIANS 4

1. What do these verses reveal about God?

2. What do these verses reveal about you?

3. What do you feel God calling you to do in response to reading these verses?

REMEMBER

The world pursues stress and hurry, but Jesus followers pursue strength and stillness through the fruit of joy.

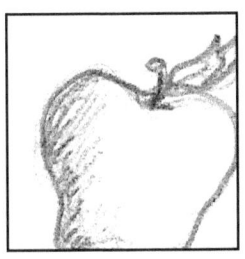

CHAPTER 4
Peace

Do you know how many times the word "peace" is used in the Bible? God says to live at peace with one another and trust Him as the provider of peace many times throughout Scripture. The word "peace" appears at least 420 times in the Bible, which indicates that when God mentions peace in Scripture, He is trying to communicate something important to us. In both the Old Testament and New Testament, peace is used to communicate who God is. In our world, peace is not easy to come by because there are so many places that suffer from an absence of peace. For example, schools, homes, and offices are common places that often lack peace. These environments can be stressful rather than peaceful when our focus moves away from God. However, we do not and should not have to settle for living in an absence of peace. As Christ-followers, we trust in the fact that Jesus is the Prince of Peace. Jesus offers His people "peace that surpasses all understanding" (Philippians 4:7). Therefore, we can bring this peace into the spaces of our lives. In the verses preceding Philippians 4:6, Paul encourages Christians not to worry. Instead, Paul invites us to pray and give thanks to God. We will talk more about this passage of Scripture in a moment, but it teaches us that even in stressful situations and seasons, God's peace is always available to us. God desires His people to lay down their worries and commit to a prayerful, grateful spirit.

Even in challenging seasons, God's gift of peace is still applicable to us. Peace is not the absence of difficulty or conflict, but instead, it is a blessing that surpasses all understanding. Christians can develop tranquil hearts because we trust that the entire world is in God's sovereign hands. Peace in Greek is the word *eriene*. This word describes peace as the absence of confusion. God's peace provides clarity in confusion. Even when we do not understand, God's peace provides direction and hope. Christians are equipped to experience peace in this life and the life to come. Peace in Hebrew is *shalom*. This means that peace is reconciliation to God. Jesus allows us to accept His peace so we can experience life free of worry. Doesn't that sound nice? A life free of worry sounds impossible, but with God, we are able to experience a peaceful life instead of a worry-filled life. The Greek and Hebrew definitions of peace remind us that God's peace surpasses our understanding. Even though our finite minds are unable to fully comprehend God's peace, let's read Scripture together to learn more.

Read these verses to learn more about God's peace:

"Peace I leave with you; my peace I give to you. Not as the world gives do I give to you. Let not your hearts be troubled, neither let them be afraid." — John 14:27 (ESV)

"I have said these things to you, that in me you may have peace. In the world, you will have tribulation. But take heart; I have overcome the world." — John 16:33 (ESV)

"And let the peace of Christ rule in your hearts, to which indeed you were called in one body. And be thankful." — Colossians 3:15 (ESV)

What do the verses above communicate about peace?

JUMPING OUT OF A PLANE

On September 5th, 2021, I decided to do something a bit crazy—I went skydiving! My mom, my dad, and my brothers came along to support and witness my experience. I was the first one in my family to skydive, so it was a new and exciting endeavor. I was even more excited because my friend, Tyra, invited me to skydive to celebrate her eighteenth birthday. Tyra and I were so excited to jump out of a plane; however, our parents were concerned—rightfully so. I tried to reassure everyone that everything was going to be okay because we would be strapped to a highly trained instructor, but everyone was still nervous even after all my attempts of persuasion. After our instructors helped us put on our harnesses, Tyra and I were ready to ride the bus to the airplane runway. We rode in a bus with fourteen other people. Then, all fourteen of us somehow squeezed into a tiny blue plane. Inside the plane, there was space for the pilot, and rather than separate seats, there were two benches. With seven people on each side of the two benches, we straddled across to fit as many people as possible. Tyra and I were next to each other and strapped against our instructors. As the plane took off, Tyra and I looked at each other with wide-eyed expressions. Then, we fixed our gaze outside through the small windows of the plane because the views were amazing. We traveled 12,500 feet high for the free fall. When it was my turn to jump, my instructor, Kyle, and I scooted toward the very edge of the plane. With one small shove, someone could have easily pushed us, and we would have fallen into the sky—that's how close to the edge of the plane we were. The side doors of the plane were wide open as our feet dangled from the edge and the wind swirled around us. After a few moments, Kyle said, "Head back!" and used his momentum to push us both off the ledge of the plane. It all happened so quickly, but Kyle and I were flying through midair within seconds. At first, I could not breathe because we were flying so quickly, but once we slowed down, I could absorb the view (and breathe) and experience the free fall. During the first forty-five seconds, I was overwhelmed and in shock. I was flying in midair for the first time ever! Once we reached a lower height, Kyle pulled the parachute cords, and we slowed down to see the incredible views. Kyle used the cords strapped to the parachute to steer our bodies to the right, then to the left, and then in circles. As we soared in the air, I was able to see the beautiful horizon and Kyle pointed out the skyline of Charlotte, NC. Skydiving was such a unique experience. I had never felt so alive in all my life! Kyle began to steer us back toward the ground and I recognized our crew cheering for us. I ran over and hugged Tyra once we both landed. We had gone skydiving—and survived! We both were so excited to have such a wonderful experience.

SKYDIVING WITH KYLE

Something I realized almost immediately was that everything would go smoothly if I chose to do tandem skydiving (where the individual skydiving is strapped to an instructor). I knew that if someone else who knew what they were doing guided me through the entire process, I would be completely fine. As I reflect on my experience,

I did not do anything to instigate the steps of the skydiving process. Instead, I listened to my instructor, Kyle, and I enjoyed the experience. I was not worried at all because I knew I could trust Kyle as a trained skydiving instructor. Kyle's abilities and knowledge gave me immense peace about the situation. Guiding people through the skydiving process has been his job for years. My abilities and knowledge would not have given me peace because I had no idea how to finesse my legs and arms into the harness I was supposed to wear. I was clueless as to how I should jump out of the plane. Additionally, I have no idea where the parachute cords were located. On my own, I would have quite literally crashed and burned, but with Kyle, I was able to free fall successfully.

In this situation, Kyle's relationship with me reminds me of God's relationship with me. Just as Kyle guided me through my first skydiving experience, God continues to guide us through our life experiences. With God as our instructor, we can obtain the fruit of the Spirit called peace. If you desire peace, look to God, because He is the only One who can give you long-lasting peace. John 14:27 (ESV) says, "Peace I leave with you; my peace I give you. I do not give to you as the world gives. Do not let your hearts be troubled and do not be afraid." Although John 14:27 instructs us not to be afraid, I will admit that I was scared before I skydived. However, Kyle saw the circumstances I was faced with and gave me the words to properly navigate the challenge. Being strapped to Kyle eased my worries, but as I approached the edge of the plane, I forgot everything Kyle had said to me before the plane ride. Kyle had prepared me for the skydiving experience very well giving me step-by-step instructions. However, once I reached the edge of the plane, I was shocked. The clouds below us were huge, and it finally hit me that I was going to jump out of the plane and soar through the sky. Because I was absorbing this new perspective and simultaneously realizing I was going to fly through the clouds below me, the words Kyle had previously said to me quickly vanished from my thoughts. As Kyle inched closer to the edge, I tried to remember Kyle's previous instructions. I thought I was surely going to mess something up because I had not remembered the instructions. Thankfully, before we jumped, Kyle reminded me exactly what I needed to hear: "Head back!" Then, we jumped out of the plane together. Kyle told me to put my head back as we jumped so that the wind would not force my head back. Putting your head back ahead of time relieves some of the shock and keeps your neck safe from whiplash. Just as Kyle reminded me of my instructions one last time before we jumped, God reminds us of what we need to hear, too. God is an instructor stronger and wiser than Kyle. Unlike Kyle, God knows each of my thoughts and can redirect them. When our minds drift, God speaks directly to us and realigns our thoughts with His and this provides peace. I felt so much better once Kyle yelled, "Head back!" When our minds wander and we need guidance, God is always ready to provide for our needs. It is helpful to remember that God communicates with us and desires to help us through every big and small season of life.

Another aspect of skydiving that gave me peace was the fact that I was strapped to Kyle. Nothing at all was separating us. Wherever I was going, Kyle was going with me. There were so many straps around me and Kyle that protected us individually, but there were specific straps that held Kyle and me together. I am so grateful I wasn't alone like the solo jumpers. I have a huge appreciation for the solo jumpers because they jump out of a plane on their own. For someone like me with little to no knowledge about skydiving, solo jumping sounds terrifying! Solo jumpers share the same knowledge as Kyle and other professional skydivers; therefore, they are able to skydive by themselves. That is so crazy to me! I was thankful I had an instructor guiding me through every step of the process. I was very grateful we were connected because knowing I was attached to Kyle shifted my focus from me to him. The same is true of God because Romans 8:38-39 (NLT) says, "I am convinced that nothing can ever separate us from God's love. Neither death nor life, neither angels nor demons, neither our fears for today nor our worries about tomorrow—not even the powers of hell can separate us from God's love. No power in the sky above or in the earth below—indeed, nothing in all creation will ever be able to separate us from the love of God that is revealed in Christ Jesus our Lord." Nothing separated me from Kyle while skydiving and nothing ever separates us from God. This knowledge gave me so much peace as I jumped out of the plane. It is important to note that the peace I felt came from me looking at Kyle. He did all the work while I watched in wonder. The same is true for our relationship with God. Peace transcends above all else in our lives when we gaze at the Prince of Peace and watch the way He works on our behalf.

> *Peace transcends above all else in our lives when we gaze at the Prince of Peace and watch the way He works on our behalf.*

Additionally, I love that I was able to experience peace as I flew in the sky. Kyle did the hard work because he pulled the parachute, directed me to various viewpoints, and landed us safely. I was simply along for the ride. It was so wonderful to feel relaxed in the midst of something so crazy and new. This is the way God works! We experience the peace of God when we let go of control and allow God to act according to His perfect plan. Giving God the ability to handle our fears, concerns, and difficulties allows for a much more enjoyable life. We can have peace when we give God the power to control our experiences. Trusting Kyle to control my skydiving experience was amazing. Can you imagine how much greater trusting God with life experiences can be? There is so much peace that comes with trusting God because when we have confidence in Him, we place our focus on someone greater than ourselves. Reliance on ourselves is untrustworthy because we are incapable of handling situations as God does. When you place your situation in God's hands, He will take care of you and overwhelm you with His abundant peace. What situations do you need to place in God's hands today?

PEACE AND SURRENDER

God's peace is different from any other because it transcends our circumstances. One morning, I felt tremendous peace as I walked outside on a beautiful day talking to God. I was in the middle of a hectic week during college. I had meetings to attend, classes throughout the day, emails to send, calls to make, texts to respond to, practices in the evenings, meals planned with friends, midterms to study for, hard decisions to make, etc. I had plenty of reasons not to experience peace. However, I could not help the fact that I was experiencing one of the most peaceful moments of my life. As I walked and prayed, I felt light on my feet and at ease in my heart. I had some bounce in my step and eagerness in my demeanor. I was not in a rush, and I felt as though I was in another dimension as busy college students rushed to class around me. The hustle and bustle of the atmosphere did not bother me, but instead, I felt calm and content. It was one of the most amazing experiences ever.

As I reflect on the heavy peace I experienced skydiving and while walking on my college campus, I thought of Philippians 4:6-7 (NIV), which says, "Do not be anxious about anything, but in every situation, by prayer and petition, with thanksgiving, present your requests to God. And the peace of God, which transcends all understanding, will guard your hearts and minds in Christ Jesus." I love this verse because it is one my parents chose for me as my life verse when I was in elementary school. I memorized this verse, and I am so thankful I have this truth in my heart and mind because it encourages me daily. My parents chose this verse for me for a number of reasons, but the main reason they decided Philippians 4:6-7 was going to be my life verse was because worries of all kinds used to consume my mind. I used to worry about safety, others' thoughts about me, and future events. Now, I know that my safety is in God's hands (Psalm 32:7), God's thoughts about me are the only ones that matter (Galatians 1:10), and God controls my future (Jeremiah 29:11).

I used to be consumed by worry, which robbed me of experiencing peace. As I studied this verse, I realized that praying and surrendering to God my requests with a thankful heart takes away the need to worry. When we realize the truth stated in Philippians 4:6 and practice this advice regularly, then we experience the truth in Philippians 4:7. The peace of God that transcends above all is gifted to us so that our hearts and minds are guarded in Christ Jesus. This verse contains beautiful words that have changed my life. As I eased out of my habit of worrying, the transcendent, unique peace of God prevailed against the worries I was facing. If you find yourself facing worry or fear, I challenge you to read and reread Philippians 4:6-7. The peace of God "transcends all understanding," which means that it has power over any of your concerns (Philippians 4:7). If you are like me and have struggled with worry or fear, know that these qualities do not define you. God desires to mark you with His peace. Surrender your concerns to Him through prayer and respond to His movement with thanks and praise.

When I was walking and praying to God on my college campus, the busyness of my life did not vanish. I still knew my day ahead was going to be chaotic, but I felt peace. I was baffled by the fact that peace could exist during such a chaotic time. However, during my walk, I was able to feel at peace even amidst the busyness because the peace of God "transcends all understanding" (Philippians 4:7). On one of the craziest days, God presented me with His peace. This was such a blessing because I needed to be reminded that God's peace is present even when our circumstances are busy. Being busy is not an excuse to rob yourself of the peace of God. In fact, God often grants us His peace in busy places because this is where we need peace the most. Although most of culture refuses to believe this, peace and our busy

> *Being busy is not an excuse to rob yourself of the peace of God.*

lives are compatible. Surrendering to God the crazy parts of our lives is the secret to experiencing His peace. God's peace is given when the world thinks peace is an impossible outcome. This explains why skydiving was so peaceful for me. Although I was intimidated and slightly scared, I ultimately felt peace because I knew I was connected to Kyle.

> *Surrendering to God the crazy parts of our lives is the secret to experiencing His peace.*

Similarly, I experienced peace during the middle of my second semester of college freshman year because I knew God was holding me tightly in His arms. God provides peace to everyone, and it is a special gift. We need to be people that cherish peace and seek to emulate it in our daily lives.

PRAY

Father,

Thank You for giving us peace that transcends all understanding. Guide me to surrender to You because Your peace is abundant, refreshing, and everlasting. Thank You for reminding us that You are the Prince of Peace. I am grateful Your peace allows me to feel protected, known, and secure. God, thank You for the immense amount of peace You pour over me. I pray that peace would surround me so that I can be led by You in all my situations. Amen.

PRAISE

Song: "Peace Be Still" by Lauren Daigle

PAUSE

1. What areas do you seek more peace in your life?

2. How can you surrender and invite God into your life so He can provide you with more of His transcending peace?

3. Who do you need to make peace with?

READ: PHILIPPIANS 4:4-9

1. What do these verses reveal about God?

2. What do these verses reveal about you?

3. What do you feel God calling you to do in response to reading these verses?

REMEMBER

The world pursues worry and doubt, but Jesus followers pursue surrender giving their burdens to God through the fruit of peace.

CHAPTER 5
Patience

Let's be honest, the practice of patience is really difficult. There is a reason why people say, "patience is a virtue." I don't want us to be intimidated as I share about the challenge of patience. Instead, I want to invite you to learn more about the blessings of patience. From the outside looking in, patience seems really difficult, but we have to remind ourselves that God is capable of helping us develop this quality. When we understand the ways God has been patient with us, it is much easier to ask God for the patience we need throughout our daily lives. Patience is difficult and will not change our circumstances immediately. However, patience does have the power to immediately change our perspectives about God, relationships, circumstances, etc. Patience is the quality that equips people to overcome adversity. It is not achieved by human strength, instead, it is accomplished through the work of the Spirit. In Greek, patience is *makrothumeo*. This means that people with patience should be able to self-restrain before proceeding to action. The Greek term shows that patience is closely related to bearing with people and giving mercy. *Savlanut* is the word for patience in Hebrew. This word includes endurance as well as steadfastness and purpose. God graciously overlooks our sins and provides forgiveness in our lives. Therefore, with patience, we should do the same with others. Patience on the surface may seem like a challenge we are unable to tackle. However, with the help of the Holy Spirit, we can learn the blessings of patience and experience them in our own lives.

After exploring the definition of patience, let's read these verses to gain better understanding:

"And let us not grow weary of doing good, for in due season we will reap if we do not give up." — Galatians 6:9 (ESV)

"But if we hope for what we do not see, we wait for it with patience." — Romans 8:25 (ESV)

"Keep your heart with all vigilance, for from it flow the springs of life." — Proverbs 4:23 (ESV)

What do the verses above communicate about patience?

STORAGE BUILDING SURPRISES

My mom's parents, who we call Nina and Papa, are from a small, country town in Georgia. My grandparents have a large storage building next to their home. For decades, they have used it to store many possessions. When we looked inside the storage building, there were numerous tubs full of dishes, books, clothing, toys, pictures, papers, and other miscellaneous items. There were also dozens of chairs, several types of furniture, five beds, and at least fifty baskets. My grandparents' storage building was full of both useful and not-so-useful items. There was such a wide variety of items, from my mom's old toys she played with when she was little to two bread cookers that had never been used. I have never seen so many strange, eclectic items all in one place. Clearly, the storage building needed some organization. Because Nina and Papa are incapable of cleaning and sorting through their storage building by themselves, my family decided to help. With six people in my family plus my two grandparents, we assumed we could easily finish the project.

However, it did not take my family very long to realize we bit off much more than we could chew. My dad and my brothers began by taking everything out from the storage building, so my mom, my sister, and I could decide whether we should throw away, donate, or keep the various items. We laid out all the items from each tub on the concrete driveway. As we unpacked boxes, the driveway to my grandparents' house was completely covered in random belongings. Organizing each tub was quite a process because the majority of the items were my grandparents' belongings;

therefore, we had to ask them their opinions about what to do with the items. I remember asking my grandma, Nina, if she needed an accordion file that I had pulled out from a large tub. I was crossing my fingers, hoping she would say no because the accordion file was torn and barely held together, but Nina said, "Hannah Beth, could you use it for school?" I thought to myself, "I cannot use an old accordion file for school," but I tried to answer her politely by saying that I use notebooks instead. My mom, my sister, and I would throw away anything too old to be used, broken, or unnecessary like the accordion file. It was beyond time to sort through all the items in the storage building.

DIFFICULTIES OF ORGANIZING

One of the most difficult parts for me during this project was pursuing patience. The word patience challenges me because it describes the capacity to accept or tolerate delay, trouble, or suffering without getting angry or upset. This fruit of the Spirit is powerful because, although patience may not immediately change our circumstances, patience immediately begins changing our hearts and our perspectives about our circumstances. Patience is arguably one of the hardest fruits of the Spirits to live out daily because it requires persistence and constant commitment. Patience is needed in many relatable circumstances. Receiving a report from the doctor, seeking a suitable partner, finding a job that suits you well, forming intimate relationships, and cleaning out a storage building all require patience. Before my family started the storage building project, I knew it was going to be difficult and time-consuming. Having patience as we sorted through boxes of books, tubs of toys, and piles of paper was challenging because it seemed like the organization process would never end. As soon as I thought my brothers and my dad had carried all the items out of the storage building, the three of them would come carrying even more items. I am someone who enjoys organizing, but I found this project entertaining only for a short while. I learned that decluttering requires an immense amount of patience. Hopefully, I will never need

> ...although patience may not immediately change our circumstances, patience immediately begins changing our hearts and our perspectives about our circumstances.

to clean out a space like my grandparents' storage building; however, this process allowed God to teach me about the condition of my spiritual life. If you haven't taken time to assess the health of your heart, you need to do so. As I cleaned and organized the storage building, I realized patience was necessary for the completion of the project. Patience is crucial as we take time to assess the health of our spiritual hearts.

The routine my family used to declutter the storage building included three options: "trash," "donate," or "keep." Decluttering our hearts is easier when we apply these same principles. For instance, I placed an item (the old accordion file I mentioned earlier) in the trash because I did not need it and no one else could benefit from its use. Most of the boxes I unpacked were kids' clothes. My grandparents do not need kids' clothes, so they allowed someone else to use them by donating them. We filled an entire trailer full of donations, but there were also some amazing items we kept. There were books of many kinds, special memories, and useful houseware that my grandparents kept because they could benefit from utilizing those resources. Like the system my family used to organize the storage building, this is a process we should use to view our hearts in God's eyes. Our hearts are made pure by Jesus Christ (Matthew 5:8) and while He calls us to guard our hearts (Proverbs 4:23), God also uniquely places His Spirit in our hearts (2 Corinthians 1:22). Because our hearts are of immense value to God, they need to become important to us too.

> *Because our hearts are of immense value to God, they need to become important to us too.*

Patience is cultivated when we take time to declutter our hearts. Oftentimes, our hearts are too full; therefore, we become impatient and hurried. We will not be patient if we are always hurrying. Patience will not fill us if our lives are too full. Patience and hurrying are incompatible. We can not live a life of patience and hurry simultaneously. To avoid a hurried life, we must commit to patience. Decluttering our lives with a patient spirit will allow us to live a slower, more intentional lifestyle. When we choose to declutter, we choose patience. Although decluttering is a challenge, it allows us to appreciate and use what God has given us. Dedication to patience will allow us to feel more refreshed and lead us to a more fulfilled way of life.

CONSIDER YOUR CURRENT STATE

Because the storage building was in a state of clutter, we realized we needed to create more space. The process of assessing what we have requires the pursuit of patience. Living in a consumer culture encourages accumulation. We like to accumulate clothes, cars, money, friends, followers, food, etc. However, if we are not creating space, everything will feel crammed, and nothing will fit properly. Determining how to make space and then resolving what items should fill that space is vital to keeping our spiritual hearts healthy. The practice of patience as we assess the health of our spiritual lives will lead us to more fulfilling lives.

REALIGN YOUR PRIORITIES

Patience is the main requirement as God helps us sort our priorities. Oftentimes, we need less distraction from the world and more devotion to the Lord. Life can be so scattered that we begin to lose sight of what is most important. Matthew 6:33 (NIV) says, "But seek first his kingdom and his righteousness, and all these things will be given to you as well." Put Him first, trust Him, and watch how He will take care of everything else in your life. Give yourself room to make changes to your priorities if needed and ask God to reshape your desires to align with His will.

GODLY TREASURE

As we assess our hearts, God will give us treasure to tuck away in our hearts. Luke 6:45 (NIV) says, "A good man brings good things out of the good stored up in his heart, and an evil man brings evil things out of the evil stored up in his heart. For the mouth speaks what the heart is full of." What we say and do reflects what is in our hearts. Matthew 6:19-21 (NIV) relates well to Luke 6:45 as it states, "Do not store up for yourselves treasures on earth, where moths and vermin destroy, and where thieves break in and steal. But store up for yourselves treasures in heaven, where moths and vermin do not destroy, and where thieves do not break in and steal. For where your treasure is, there your heart will be also." In our hearts, there

> *Continually asking God to fill our hearts with the treasures of His Word keeps our spiritual hearts healthy.*

should be heavenly treasures—not earthly ones. Continually asking God to fill our hearts with the treasures of His Word keeps our spiritual hearts healthy.

REORGANIZATION CREATES TRANSFORMATION

Unfortunately, my family will most likely have to clean out the storage building again—maybe not to the extent of the first time, but all spaces require maintenance. Expect to maintain the areas of your heart as well. Cleaning and organizing never happen just once because we continue to accumulate items without sorting through them. For example, I often organize the pantry or the refrigerator at my house. The constant accumulation and depletion of items creates a need for reorganization. This process requires patience as it is challenging and time-consuming. However, the before and after stages of this process look completely different because the space was transformed. We can transform spaces like a storage building or a refrigerator, but only God can transform hearts. When we pursue patience, God pursues transformation.

Our desires should reflect a longing to see God pursue transformation on the inside of us. Organizing our hearts is not a task to complete so that we look "put together" because ultimately, no one is "put together." Being "put together" can appear real, but sin has shattered our hearts because "There is no one righteous, not even one; there is no one who understands; there is no one who seeks God" (Romans 9:11). No one is capable of being righteous (or "put together") because only Christ remains unstained by sin. Being cleansed from sin isn't about looking nicer on the outside. The Lord cares most deeply about transformation on the inside. 1 Samuel 16:7 (NIV) says, "But the Lord said to Samuel, 'Do not consider his appearance or his height, for I have rejected him.' The Lord does not look at the things people look at. People look at the outward appearance, but the Lord looks at the heart."

It is important for us to remember that we depend on God alone for the true acts of transformation. Patience to depend on the Lord is crucial to successfully fulfilling His purpose for our lives. Unorganized items do not serve a purpose, but when God reorganizes the desires of our hearts, He grants us a purpose—loving God and loving people (Matthew 22:36-40). We are made new so that we can embrace our God-given purpose. God wants to use you, so ask Him for patience as He shapes you to become more like Him.

PATIENCE AND INTENTIONALITY

Throwing away is not easy; however, the reason we throw away is to create room to intentionally add something of greater value. For example, you only throw away trash because it is the remainder of an item that is no longer needed. Things of greater value can be added when things of lesser value are thrown away. We should desire that our hearts become more God-honoring, so throwing away too much screen time, bad relationships, or negative commitments creates space in our hearts. This gives us more opportunity to treasure essential items like God's Word, prayer, and worship. Keep the presence of God, the presence of uplifting friends, and the presence of comforting family members. Treasure people, places, or things in your life that draw you closer to God and equip you to honor Him. The goal of intentionally assessing our hearts is to draw closer to the Lord in understanding His will for us individually as believers and collectively as members of His Kingdom.

I realize intentionally assessing your heart is a big project like cleaning the storage building, but God gives patience so that we can handle larger and more important assignments. God also tells us that there is a time for everything: there is a time to keep and a time to throw away (Ecclesiastes 3:6). It is important to prioritize intentionally assessing your heart, but don't feel like you need to rush through the process, because like the storage building process, it takes time. Being careful and thoughtful as you consider the condition of your heart and the place for the items within your heart is important. Take your time as you process, but do not wait to start the process. The process of organizing the storage building should have happened years ago, but because we waited, more items accumulated. This made the process much more difficult. The quicker you can start and the more consistent you can be in intentionally assessing the conditions of your heart, the healthier you will be. Slowing down and pursuing patience will allow you and me to bear healthy, godly fruit as the Holy Spirit works in our hearts.

PRAY

Dear God,
Patience is very difficult, but will You please help me be patient in every circumstance? Challenge me and bring me closer to You. Help me look more like You as I learn about patience. Please give me intentional patience as I assess the areas of my heart. Align my will with Your will. Help me to be patient with others and thank You for being patient with me. Amen.

PRAISE

Song: "Make Room" by The Church Will Sing, Elyssa Smith, and Community Music

PAUSE

1. What are areas of your heart that you need to reorganize?

2. How can you intentionally reorganize without simply doing so to look "put together?"

3. What can you throw away, share, and keep to maintain a healthy heart?

READ: ECCLESIASTES 3:1-8

1. What do these verses reveal about God?

2. What do these verses reveal about you?

3. What do you feel God calling you to do in response to reading these verses?

REMEMBER

The world pursues accumulation of temporary pleasures, but Jesus followers pursue godly treasures through the fruit of patience.

CHAPTER 6
Kindness

There are not many things that have a greater influence in our world than kindness. I can think of many examples where kindness from others has blessed me. Has anyone ever spoken a kind word to you that you needed right in that moment? Have you ever been surprised by a gift left on your doorstep, a meal prepared for you, a note left in your room, or any other random act of kindness? It amazes me how kindness can come in both big and small packages, yet the impact is the same—kindness changes people. Kindness has the ability to affect our words, thoughts, and actions. People who are consistently kind have a different demeanor. They think of others before themselves and desire to encourage others. Kindness is the ability to treat others like Christ does. Kindness brings out God's character within members of His Kingdom. In Greek, kindness is *chrestos*. Kindness is often correlated with philanthropy and displays grace, harmlessness, and wisdom. Similarly, kindness in Hebrew is *gemilut chasadim*, which can also be stated as the practice of love. Kindness is greater than simply doing the right thing. Kindness is caring for others' needs out of genuine concern and compassion.

Please read the verses below for a greater understanding of God's kindness:

"Be kind to one another, tenderhearted, forgiving one another, as God in Christ forgave you." — Ephesians 4:32 (ESV)

"But love your enemies, and do good, and lend, expecting nothing in return, and your reward will be great, and you will be sons of the Most High, for he is kind to the ungrateful and the evil." — Luke 6:35 (NIV)

"A man who is kind benefits himself, but a cruel man hurts himself." —Proverbs 11:17 (ESV)

What do the verses above communicate about kindness?

TEA TIME

Have you ever been to an English high tea with teacups, scones, and fancy attire? My answer to this question, until my senior year of high school, was no. However, I had the opportunity to attend a tea party before I graduated high school. One of my mom's closest friends, Mrs. Priscilla, graciously offered to host a tea party for my friends and me to celebrate our senior year. When I arrived for the tea party, Mrs. Priscilla had beautiful flowery tablecloths, trays of gourmet foods (sandwiches, quiches, fruit, desserts, etc.), and sherbet floats for each guest. She had arranged everything perfectly and I was so impressed! Everyone wore beautiful dresses and fancy hats, and I loved seeing how gorgeous all my friends looked in their tea party outfits! My mom, Mrs. Priscilla, and our sweet neighbor, Mrs. Sue, served me and my friends as we enjoyed the delicacies of the tea party. I am amazed at how wonderful this experience was for me and my friends!

Once everyone finished eating, my mom talked about how she recognized the value of tea in our lives as Christians. My mom encouraged us in a way I was not expecting. She paralleled our lives as Christians to a tea bag. It sounded strange to me at first, but pay close attention as I explain her words so you can better understand God's kindness: My mom explained how water is plain and flavorless; however, once a tea bag is dipped into the water, immense amounts of flavor begin to permeate the liquid. I thought about tea bags and how there are many variations of tea. Some of my favorites are green tea, jasmine tea, and lavender tea. Each type of tea has different flavors that make their taste unique. Tea adds flavor to the water as the tea bag filled with herbs and spices permeates the liquid. I was reminded that I have many types of friends, and just like tea, each one of my friends enhances different aspects of my life. Some of my friends are better at encouraging me, while others are skilled in the way they listen. I have friends that make me smile and laugh, but I also have friends who remain constant in challenging seasons. My friends also enjoy a variety of activities like running, singing, and cooking. The parallel between tea and my friends powerfully struck me because I noticed that if we are all tea bags, we have the potential to flavor others' lives. It doesn't matter where our interests lie, what our passions are, or what our personalities say about us. All that matters is that we are intentional with enhancing our God-given flavor in others' lives.

One of the many important lessons of the Bible is that we desperately need each other. Corinthians 12:21 (NIV) says, "The eye cannot say to the hand, 'I don't need you!' And the head cannot say to the feet, 'I don't need you!'" This proves that for each of us to succeed, we need support from people with different God-given gifts. Although the eye and the feet are different body parts with different functions, they still depend on one another. Verses 26-27 continue, "If one part suffers, every part suffers with it; if one part is honored, every part rejoices with it. Now you are the body of Christ, and each one of you is a part of it." As a community, we are called to rejoice with those who rejoice and mourn with those who mourn (Romans 12:15). Each of us brings different flavors like a tea bag; however, when we help each other, we become a reflection of the body of Christ. Relating to others in seasons of joy and sorrow allows for the body of Christ to become strong and solidified. The ideas from 1 Corinthians 12 and Romans 12 both remind me of a key characteristic God mentions repeatedly in His Word: kindness.

Kindness is a flavor I seek to enhance in my life. Being friendly, generous, and considerate are all qualities that describe the fruit of the Spirit known as kindness. I am blessed to know many kind people. The friends with me at the senior tea party have been consistently kind to me. Also, my mom's friend, Mrs. Priscilla, assembled the entire tea party for me and my friends to enjoy. She lives a very busy life as a mom of three children, yet she found time to plan and prepare an elegant tea party. Mrs. Priscilla insisted on hosting a tea party for me and allowed it to be one of her top priorities at the end of the school year. She desired to put together a tea party because of the genuine kindness God placed in her heart. I am more inspired and overwhelmed with gratitude knowing that Mrs. Priscilla prepared and hosted the senior tea party after recovering from cancer. Although it had been almost a year since her recovery, her daily life looks drastically different. The challenges she faces daily did not stop her from pursuing kindness towards me and I deeply admire her for that! Kindness can't be limited due to difficulty. If you are willing to surrender your hardships to God, He will bless you with His kindness and show you how to share it with others in a God-honoring way.

Kindness can't be limited due to difficulty.

THE PERFECT GRADUATION GIFT

One of the kindest people I know lived right next door to my family when we lived in North Carolina. My previous neighbor, Mrs. Sue, exemplifies kindness in everything she says and does. She has brought sweet treats for my family, watched our crazy dog while we are on vacation, and she has been there to encourage my family in all our activities—dance, running, football, you name it! Mrs. Sue is so intentional with her words and always uses them to lift me up. She also uses her various God-given gifts to show others kindness. Mrs. Sue attended the senior tea party Mrs. Priscilla hosted for me and she was excited to help serve and did so with a grateful heart. One memory I will never forget occurred before my high school graduation party. Mrs. Sue was at my house a few hours early to help organize the food and activities for the party at our house. She and I bagged popcorn for forty-five minutes together. How kind of Mrs. Sue to dedicate her time to me and my graduation party!

After we finished setting up for the graduation party, Mrs. Sue brought over a huge basket with my graduation gift. Little did I know, a gift I will forever treasure was inside the basket. Mrs. Sue hand-made a quilt composed of my T-shirts from my 6th–12th grade years for my graduation gift. There were so many special memories tied together through the quilt Mrs. Sue created. As I looked at the quilt, I reminisced over my middle and high school years. Mrs. Sue worked endlessly for the entirety of my senior year to present me with this gift. It was evident she worked hard because each T-shirt was cut into squares and stitched together so nicely. As soon as I opened Mrs. Sue's gift, I could immediately sense she invested large amounts of time, effort, and energy into this massive project. The beautiful quilt Mrs. Sue made for me now sits in a special place in my room. Every time I see it, I sense how the quality of kindness is beautifully portrayed through people like Mrs. Sue. I realized that kindness is explained and displayed wonderfully through a quilt. Just as a quilt is made of different patterns and shapes, kindness comes in all forms and fashions. When I looked at all my T-shirts from 6th–12th grade separately, I did not think they matched or coordinated. I would have never thought combining all my T-shirts could make an amazing, coherent quilt. However, Mrs. Sue weaved each part together intentionally, which created the perfect graduation gift. The same is true with kindness. Like a quilt, it comes in different sizes and styles, but God uses kindness to sew all parts of our lives together. Kindness has the power to create an inspiring portrait for all to admire, pointing people to Christ. The core of kindness is found within our Savior, Jesus Christ.

> *The core of kindness is found within our Savior, Jesus Christ.*

KINDNESS ON THE CROSS

King Jesus is the embodiment of kindness. Jesus exudes kindness in every way; however, right before His death, four crucial moments of kindness are highlighted in Scripture. In Luke 23, Jesus carried His cross and passed people in the crowd on His way to the place of His crucifixion. As Jesus walked, there were women who were weeping for Him as He prepared for His death. Jesus talked to the women and told them not to weep for Him. Jesus was kind by warning them of the future troubles the nation would walk through. Jesus stopped to warn these women and showed kindness as He gave them information about their future. The timing of this interaction is important to note because Jesus was carrying a heavy cross while being yelled at by His persecutors. During all this commotion, Jesus stopped to talk to weeping women.

Jesus continued to demonstrate kindness as He was nailed to the cross. Jesus's body was weak, bloody, and beaten; however, Jesus began to talk to His Father despite His painful circumstances. Jesus asked for forgiveness on behalf of the executioners and tormentors that did not believe His identity as the Son of God. Jesus talked to God and explained that if the people knew He was the Messiah, they would not have treated Him in such a horrific way. Jesus, through extreme kindness, intervened on behalf of every sinner. Jesus asked for forgiveness for those who deeply hurt Him and nailed Him to the cross to die. Clearly, these individuals did not deserve forgiveness; however, Jesus knew they needed a cleansed heart and kindly asked the Father to wash their sins away.

As Jesus was breathing His last breaths on the cross and aching in pain, the men on either side of Him were talking. They asked Jesus to save Himself and wondered if He was truly the Messiah. The conversation continued and the thief nailed to the cross next to Jesus realized that Jesus was an innocent man. Because the thief recognized Jesus's identity as the righteous Savior of the world, God blessed him with salvation and assured that he would dwell in heaven with Christ forever. Jesus spread the Father's kindness until He breathed His very last breath. In John 19, we notice that before Jesus died, He showed kindness to Mary (His mother), Mary Magdalene, and His mother's sister-in-law (also named Mary) by ensuring they were taken care of. The three women named Mary were concerned for Jesus during His suffering and Jesus showed kindness toward each one of them. Mary (Jesus's mother), Mary Magdalene, and Mary (Jesus's mom's sister-in-law) were with Jesus during His last hour. They were at the cross to support Him when He was the one supporting them by ensuring they would be safe after He departed from the earth into heaven.

Jesus's kindness is evident as He cared not only for women weeping (Luke 23:28), but He cares deeply for you and me (Isaiah 43:2). Jesus not only offered forgiveness to the executioners and tormentors (Luke 23:34), but He offers forgiveness to you and me (Psalm 103:10-12). Jesus not only leads thieves on the cross to salvation (Luke 23:39), but Jesus also leads people like you and me, too (John 14:6). Jesus did not only ensure that the three Marys would be taken care of (John 19:26), but He ensured you and I would be taken care of as well (Psalm 34:7-9). Jesus died for every single human being and that is the true definition of kindness (John 3:16). No one is deserving of a Savior, but Jesus died for us because He knew no one else was equipped with the kindness He had received from the Father as He came to earth with a mission to reconcile our hearts to Him.

KINDNESS AND GENEROSITY

Kindness is displayed in many ways; however, it is frequently displayed through generosity. For example, in the examples I shared, Mrs. Priscilla and Mrs. Sue gave their time and resources to celebrate me during my senior year. Giving is a huge aspect of kindness because giving to someone shows that you care about them and desire the best for them. Mrs. Priscilla cared for me so much that she arranged an entire tea party for me and my friends. She had never met any of my friends before; however, since she cared for me, she also cared for the friends in my life. I know that she desires the best for me because of her genuine care and kindness for me and my friends. Also, I am very grateful for the way Mrs. Sue cares for me. She spent time helping me prepare for my graduation party, which was a gift in and of itself. However, she also cared enough about me to give me a sweet and special quilt for graduation. Mrs. Priscilla spent days preparing for the tea party while Mrs. Sue spent an entire year working on my quilt and dedicated several hours at my house setting up for my graduation party. Jesus showed kindness on the cross by giving up His life for our sake. That is ultimately what kindness is all about. Generosity is a primary way to reflect God's kindness.

Proverbs 3:3 (NLT) says, "Never let loyalty and kindness leave you! Tie them around your neck as a reminder. Write them deep within your heart." Writing kindness deep within our hearts allows kindness not to be a superficial characteristic, but a defining quality rooted deeply in our hearts. Listen to the Lord's promptings in your life and He will open doors for you to spread His kindness to others. Like oxygen, kindness is needed in everyone's life, so let God equip you to spread kindness generously to change the world around you.

Listen to the Lord's promptings in your life and He will open doors for you to spread His kindness to others.

PRAY

King Jesus,
Thank You for being the ultimate example of kindness. Help me follow Your example as I learn more about the quality of kindness and how to embody it daily. God, I thank You for the people that have been kind to me, and I pray that You would equip me to be generously kind to others. I am blessed by Your kindness, and I am overwhelmed by its abundance in my life. Lord Jesus, help me to spread kindness everywhere I go so that Your name may be given the glory it deserves. Amen.

PRAISE

Song: "Living Hope" by Phil Wickham

PAUSE

1. Who is God calling you to show kindness to?

2. How can you carry generosity and kindness with you every day?

3. How can you learn kindness from Jesus?

READ: PROVERBS 3:3-6

1. What do these verses reveal about God?

2. What do these verses reveal about you?

3. What do you feel God is calling you to do in response to reading these verses?

REMEMBER

The world pursues selfish ambition, but Jesus followers pursue selfless acts of generosity through the fruit of kindness.

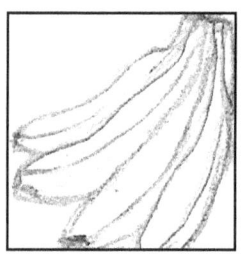

CHAPTER 7
Goodness

Have you ever been told by your parents, "Be good!" My parents used to tell me this all the time and sometimes I wondered, would they ever one day shout, "Be bad!" I laugh at this childhood thought, but it's true that parents care about the behaviors of their children. I realized my parents never wanted me to behave badly, so they always reminded me to "be good" instead. As I left for school, a friend's house, or piano lessons, they always reminded me to "be good." They did this to help me remember to have polite and respectful behavior around others. As a kid, I never questioned what my parents meant when they told me to "be good." I knew that they desired me to be on my best behavior, use proper manners, and be kind to others. My parents set clear expectations for what it meant to "be good." It amazes me that at a young age we have a fairly clear understanding of good and bad, whether we learn the difference from our parents, friends, or culture. Parents often reward their kids for good behavior and punish them for bad behavior, which classifies behaviors into categories for children to understand what they ought to do and not do. The classification for "good" as a child is only a fraction of true goodness in the world because goodness describes more than behavior. As Christians, we learn through Scripture that goodness is a way of life. Goodness involves the way we speak, act, and think. It more importantly includes reflecting on our good God by giving Him praise and thanks. Goodness is seen in a person that reflects Christ's character and values. Those who are good understand God's goodness and seek to imitate Him in their words, thoughts, and actions. Goodness in Greek is *agathos*.

This means "active goodness" and it portrays someone doing good deeds. These deeds are ones that need to be accomplished and not merely thought of or intended. God's goodness is one that follows through. In Hebrew, the word for "good" is *tov*. This word describes goodness as tenderheartedness and generosity. Goodness is fulfilled through compassion and giving to God's people as Jesus does. Let's take a closer look at the goodness of God together.

Read the verses below to experience a testament to God's goodness through Scripture:

"Oh, taste and see that the Lord is good! Blessed is the man who takes refuge in him!" — Psalm 34:8 (NLT)

"Oh, how abundant is your goodness, which you have stored up for those who fear you and worked for those who take refuge in you, in the sight of the children of mankind!" — Psalm 31:19 (ESV)

"I remain confident of this: I will see the goodness of the Lord in the land of the living. Wait for the Lord; be strong and take heart and wait for the Lord." — Psalm 27: 13-14 (NIV)

What do the verses above communicate about goodness?

PARTY OF SIX

Eleven years ago, God led my family to adopt my brother, Muntu, from the Democratic Republic of the Congo (DRC). My family desired to adopt partially because my mom could not have any more children after my youngest brother, Noah, was born. God had already blessed my mom with three children, but she knew our family was not complete. After a few months of praying about adoption, my family was in agreement and knew God had called us to adopt. We desired to adopt a boy around the age of five to match the age of my brother, Noah, at the time. Our social worker showed my family a picture of my brother, Muntu, and we immediately fell in love with his amazing smile. We had never met Muntu before, but we felt that God was calling us to invite this boy from the DRC into our family. Many people warned us against adoption from the DRC because of its mass corruption. We understood the concern and care of our friends and family, but God so clearly matched our family with Muntu in the DRC. We desperately desired for Muntu to join our family and we loved him so much that his location was not a factor in our decision. The fact that Muntu lived in the DRC was not his fault and he needed help like many other orphans in the world. God led us to adopt, but we did not realize the process would take three years. We started the adoption journey when he was five years old, but Muntu was eight years old when he finally arrived in America. Our journey was longer because the paperwork took time to complete, the DRC government closed its doors during our process, and planning for adoption requires intentional effort and preparation. Many people began to question if we were still adopting because it took much longer than expected. However, I learned a huge lesson about waiting patiently and praying fervently during those long three years. In April of 2016, my parents finally received news that they could travel to the DRC to bring Muntu home. Although the DRC is dangerous, my parents boldly trusted in the Lord for security, guidance, strength, and protection. Finally, on May 2, 2016, Muntu entered the Brown family and arrived at his new home in America. Any one of my family members would tell you that Muntu was the missing puzzle piece we were searching for to complete our family. I am so grateful to say that compared to most adoptions, our experience was smooth and easy. Muntu adjusted to his new home, family, and environment very quickly. We are so blessed God united Muntu from the DRC with our family in the U.S.

AN UNBELIEVABLE MESSAGE

About five years after adopting Muntu, my mom received an unbelievable Facebook message. A lady reached out to my mom saying she believed that her adopted son, Kaleb, was related to my adopted brother, Muntu. The possibility of Muntu having a connection with a biological sibling was exciting for our entire family. However, entering this relationship, we realized we needed to be careful because the corruption within my brother's birthplace makes it very difficult to determine honest situations. People have reached out to my parents on other occasions claiming that they are his relatives. We do not want to automatically assume these people are untruthful, but we had to enter each scenario with caution. Initially, my family was unsure if the circumstances regarding Kaleb were trustworthy. However, my parents asked Kaleb's family specific questions about his life to see if their memories aligned. We believed the two boys may have a true connection, so to bring clarity to the situation, Muntu completed a 23 and Me DNA test. This would give us accurate information to determine whether or not Kaleb and Muntu were related.

After a few weeks, my family received news regarding Muntu's DNA test. To our surprise, Kaleb and Muntu were not related; however, my family discovered Muntu had a half-sister. This was not news we expected to hear, but we were so excited to discover Muntu had another relative. My mom immediately contacted the family who adopted Muntu's half-sister. We received a quick response from her family, and we learned Muntu's half-sister's name is Anistyn. She is one year older than Muntu and her family lives in Missouri. At the time my family discovered Muntu and Anistyn's connection, Anistyn's family was on vacation in Myrtle Beach, S.C. Our home is much closer to Myrtle Beach than it is to Missouri, so we decided to meet Anistyn and her family while they were close by.

REBEL PIE

My family drove two hours to meet Anistyn and her family for dinner at a pizza place called Rebel Pie. As soon as we arrived, we embraced their family with hugs. Meeting Muntu's half-sister and her family was a surreal moment. It felt like something out of a movie! It was such a blessing we were able to connect with Anistyn and her family. Anistyn and Muntu were more alike than I expected. At dinner, we learned that like Muntu, Anistyn loves food and sports. Also, Muntu and Anistyn share similar features. They share the same joyful smile, big personality, bright eyes, and curly hair. Our time together with Anistyn's family was so special.

During his first five years in Africa, Muntu has little remembrance of his biological mother; however, he vividly remembers details of his father. At the age of five, Muntu remembers being on a boat with his dad and his sister. They first used a small boat (probably a raft) to float down a river. Then, they transferred to a bigger boat with more people. Muntu's family at that time was trying to escape from the civil war in their area. Anistyn recalls this memory too. Our family and Anistyn's family assume that Muntu and Anistyn share the same father. From gathering details from their history, we also believe that their father sent Anistyn away, because she remembers being sick after they fled to Kinshasa on the boats. Anistyn was placed in a foster home once she recovered from illness while Muntu was still with his father. Muntu was five years old when his father became ill. One day, Muntu said he went to check on his dad and found him lifeless in his bed. Five-year-old Muntu did the only thing he knew to do and ran to the church across the street for help. Members of the church took his father's body and buried it. Muntu witnessed his father's death and had no known relatives who could take care of him. After the death of his father, Muntu was sent to an orphanage. Shortly after Muntu arrived at the orphanage, my family discovered him through our social worker. Unlike Muntu, Anistyn never went to an orphanage, but she lived with a foster family. She arrived in America when she was eleven years old. Muntu and Anistyn's backgrounds make our families' connection even more of a blessing! It blows my mind that Muntu and Anistyn were together on a raft and on a boat in the Congo River when they were little, but now that they are older, both of them live in the U.S. and could reconnect at a pizza place!

God's goodness is all the more amazing because even though not everyone was adopted or an orphan like my brother, everyone has a spot available to them within God's family. In fact, we were orphans before God made us His own. However, God in His great goodness gave each of us belonging and acceptance through Christ. Jesus serves as the bridge from God the Father to God's people. Therefore, because Jesus lived a righteous life no human being could ever live, He tasted death for all humanity. Christ sacrificed His life so that we could be made one with the Lord. Despite our sin, God sees us the same way He sees Jesus. When Jesus died on the cross, we died to our sinful nature. When Jesus rose from the dead, we rose from our sinful life into a new life in Christ. Because of this beautiful transformation, God adopts us into His family. God gives His children names and He intentionally provides purpose for each one of His people. Therefore, God's goodness reaches you and has been running after you since the moment you were created. God is always good and we can remind ourselves of this truth by remembering His work on the cross to save us from our sins.

GOD'S GOODNESS YIELDS PERSEVERANCE

My family originally thought Muntu had a brother, and we were disappointed when that relationship was proved non-existent by the DNA results. However, God blessed us by providing the amazing news that Muntu had a half-sister! We would have never known about Anistyn and her family if it weren't for the way God placed Kaleb in our lives. God used a quick disappointment with Kaleb to lead us to something greater. Muntu and Anistyn's story is one of many displays of God's goodness.

God's goodness is unlike any other. God remains good even though our circumstances may not always be described as good. For example, Muntu's birthplace is very broken. Neither Muntu nor my family could imagine anything good coming from his situation before he arrived in America. We do not know what happened to Muntu's mom, but we presume that she died when Muntu was young because he has no recollection of her. Muntu's father died when Muntu was five years old due to sickness. Then, he was sent to an orphanage in one of the most poverty-stricken cities in the world and was almost rotated out of the orphanage due to overcrowding. Thankfully, God's goodness prevailed, and He used my family to rescue Muntu from the darkness that surrounded his life. There is a mystery about God's goodness because sometimes we are unable to see it, but that does not hinder the fact that it is always present. One of the wonderful aspects of God's goodness is that we do not deserve it, yet He overflows our lives with it constantly whether we realize it or not.

> God remains good even though our circumstances may not always be described as good.

> There is a mystery about God's goodness because sometimes we are unable to see it, but that does not hinder the fact that it is always present.

It is difficult having Anistyn and her family living so far away; however, I have noticed that when my relationships are grounded within God's goodness, they are much healthier and last longer despite factors like distance. Even though Anistyn lives hours away from my family, I am trusting that the Lord will keep strengthening our relationship with their family. I love that God's goodness works beyond our human limitations. He brought two families together and if it weren't for His mighty work, neither of our families would have ever known that we were connected through Muntu and Anistyn.

God brought Muntu into our family nine years ago, Anistyn into her family seven years ago, and both families together five years ago. God's timing is perfect, and I am so grateful God promises in Romans 8:28 (ESV) that "all things work for the good of those who love Him and are called according to His purposes." Only God can bridge lives together in such an impactful way. Muntu and Anistyn's stories include scenarios that seem impossible and obstacles that seem unbeatable. Challenges like the ones Muntu and Anistyn faced are ones that cannot be conquered without God's prevailing goodness. The goodness of God has the power to unite, grow, and sustain relationships. The goodness of God has the power to overcome troublesome circumstances. The goodness of God has the power to turn broken stories into beautiful stories. God's goodness is not only reserved for Muntu and Anistyn because His goodness is abundant and never-ending. God seeks to reveal His goodness every day. If you pray, asking God to reveal His goodness to you, God will begin opening your eyes and heart to allow you to recognize the immense power in His goodness. Look at the ways God spreads His goodness to you. You may be surprised as goodness often appears in unexpected places and times. Regardless of the way God reveals His goodness to you, remember to give Him glory for the goodness He pours over you.

> *God seeks to reveal His goodness every day.*

PRAY

Almighty God,
You are so good. Thank You for being good in the hardest of situations. Remind me that Your goodness always prevails. Sometimes, I am unable to see Your goodness, but remind me to open my eyes to see Your goodness in a new way today. Amen.

PRAISE

Song: "Evidence" by Josh Baldwin

PAUSE

1. Where do you see God's goodness in your life today?

2. How has God been good to you in the past?

3. How can you share the goodness of God with others?

READ: PSALM 23

1. What do these verses reveal about God?

2. What do these verses reveal about you?

3. What do you feel God calling you to do in response to reading these verses?

REMEMBER

The world pursues victory over hardship without hope, but Jesus followers pursue perseverance through challenges with hope through the fruit of goodness.

CHAPTER 8
Faithfulness

The quality of faithfulness amazes me because although we may not see faithfulness in the moment, when we look back, we more clearly see God's hand in our circumstances. I admit that there have been countless times where I have questioned God's faithfulness. Will God prove faithful this time? Will He provide in my situation? Does God see me? However, God never fails, which means His faithfulness never falls short. Although time after time I have been unfaithful, God relentlessly pursues you and me with His faithfulness that never ends. Faithfulness describes the quality of being reliable and trustworthy. This is not achieved by heroic virtue, but instead, it is a byproduct of the Spirit. "Faithfulness" in Greek is *pisteos*. Faith is a firm persuasion or conviction of truth. The Hebrew word for faithfulness is *ne'emunut*. This refers to trustworthiness and dependability. The Holy Spirit enables the heart to be a safe source of counsel and strength for other people. God is ultimately faithful; therefore, He equips His people to be faithful as well.

The verses that follow will provide you and I with a deeper understanding of biblical faith:

"For we walk by faith, not by sight." — 2 Corinthians 5:7: (ESV)

"A faithful man will abound with blessings, but whoever hastens to be rich will not go unpunished." — Proverbs 28:20 (NIV)

"When you pass through the waters, I will be with you; and through the rivers, they shall not overwhelm you; when you walk through fire

you shall not be burned, and the flame shall not consume you."
— Isaiah 43:2 (ESV)

What do these verses communicate about faithfulness?

EAR INFECTION

It was the summer of 2021. I had just returned from a five-day mission trip in South Dakota. I had to regroup after being away from home for a few days, so I was catching up on some of my responsibilities. However, I could not focus because my right ear started to bother me. I initially thought it could be from the plane ride the day before, but because my ear was not getting better, I had a feeling my ear trouble was resulting from an ear infection. Because I have experienced the pain of an ear infection numerous times, I told my parents and they advised that I go to urgent care so I could confirm it was an ear infection and receive antibiotics. When I arrived at urgent care, I told the doctor I had been having some trouble with my right ear. He looked in both of my ears and said that I had an ear infection in the right ear, and one was starting to form in the left ear. Thankfully, the doctor prescribed me some antibiotics and I left to go pick them up at the pharmacy.

LOST ON THE INTERSTATE

I called my mom to update her about my appointment and as I finished the conversation, I warned her that my phone may die. I was not aware until I looked down at my screen that my phone was at only 3% when I left urgent care. I had a charger cord in my car; however, I realized it no longer worked. Although I knew the way from urgent care to CVS, I figured there was a quicker way to arrive due to the constant traffic in Charlotte, NC. The GPS guided me toward the interstate. I knew my phone was going to die shortly, but once I started recognizing the names and numbers on the upcoming exit signs, I knew I would know where I was going. But counter to what I had told myself, as I was driving on the interstate, I realized that I did not recognize any of the exit signs I passed. I glanced at my GPS to double-check my location and suddenly, my music and maps turned off because my phone died. I immediately panicked, but I tried to stay calm as I searched for anything familiar as I drove. I saw nothing that caught my attention and after a few minutes, I decided it would be best to pull off the interstate at the next exit so I could figure out what to do. I drove down an unfamiliar road for what felt like a very long time. I was looking for any kind of building or parking lot I could pull into. I was thankful I passed a "Charlotte City Limit" sign. At least I was still in Charlotte somewhere, but nothing about where I was driving seemed familiar. Finally, I saw a CVS—not the CVS near my house where I was supposed to pick up my medicine—but it was still a CVS. I didn't recognize any of the other places nearby, but I parked my car in the parking lot. I thought to myself, "What am I going to do?" After desperately contemplating for a couple of minutes, I realized my car has a GPS system built into its software. My hands were shaking and my head was pounding, but I finally figured out how to work my car's GPS system and I typed in my home address. I pulled out of the CVS parking lot and carefully listened to my GPS as I drove. On the way home, I was running low on gas, it started raining, and my ear was painfully pounding. However, I did start to recognize a few exit signs on the interstate after a short while. I was the definition of a "crash and burn." As I was driving home, I heard a whisper of truth: "Do not be afraid. I am with you." These words are so powerful, and they reminded me that I know God is with me. Even though my phone died, and I couldn't communicate with my parents, friends, or anyone about this situation, I could talk to God because He was right there. He never left my side during my crazy journey. As God was speaking to me, I finally made it to a familiar exit, and I confidently knew my way home. Although this was a crazy experience, God taught me more about His divine faithfulness.

GOD'S FAITHFULNESS TO ME

God spoke to me while I was driving on the interstate and said: "Do not be afraid. I am with you." This statement from God reminded me that He is faithful in all circumstances. Whether you are confused, lonely, scared, lost, or all of the above like I was, God remains faithful. Faithfulness is the fruit of the Spirit that means being faithful or remaining true to your word. God pointed me to the truth that says, "Do not be afraid. I am with you." These words struck me at that moment differently than ever before because I was in a position where I desperately needed to hear them. I was in the car alone and lost with no one to turn to other than God. Usually, I meditate on this truth when I am comfortable and safe in my room. When I am in my room, I am not afraid because I know where I am. However, when my phone died, I panicked. My fear arose from the knowledge that I was alone, I didn't know where to go, and had no way of communicating with anyone about my circumstances. Then, God called my name and reminded me of His divine presence and faithfulness.

I have heard the phrase, "Do not be afraid, I am with you," since I was a little girl in Sunday school, but it wasn't until this moment that this truth deeply settled in my heart. The benefit of understanding Scripture is key because understanding leads to application. Applying Scripture helps us become more familiar with our faithful God. For instance, in my situation, God spoke Scripture over my heart, and I was reminded of God's faithfulness even during my chaotic moment of panic. Even though I was filled with fear, reflecting on this moment allowed me to be grateful for my journey on the interstate because I experienced His words come to life. God's faithfulness doesn't depend on circumstances. God helps us understand His faithfulness in our circumstances, but God's faithfulness is not determined through our circumstances. He is always faithful, and we have the blessing of recognizing that truth, sharing it with others, and walking in freedom.

He is always faithful, and we have the blessing of recognizing that truth, sharing it with others, and walking in freedom.

FAITHFUL MEN AND WOMEN OF THE BIBLE

Faithfulness is a rare quality because it requires never-ending devotion and intentional pursuit. In Hebrews 11, many people in God's Word are remembered for their faith in God. When I think of people who are faithful, I like to break down the word as "faith-full" because people who are faithful are full of faith. Hebrews 11 is such an incredible passage because it beautifully highlights the way God blessed His people when they placed their faith in Him. God never says that being faithful will be easy; however, God shows that being faithful promises benefits in this life and the life to come. In Hebrews 11, we learn that by faith, Biblical characters were honored by God. By faith, Abel brought a better offering than Cain and was considered righteous (verse 4). By faith, Enoch was taken from life on earth so that he did not have to experience death (verses 5-6). By faith, Noah built an ark for his family and remained obedient to God (verse 7). By faith, Abraham left his hometown, followed God into the unknown, blessed many nations, and endured testing from God. (verses 8-10, 12-19). By faith, Sarah gave birth even though she had passed the normal age to bear a child (verse 11). By faith, Isaac blessed Jacob and Esau (verse 20). By faith, Jacob blessed Joseph's sons as he died (verse 21). By faith, Joseph spoke about the exodus of the Israelites from Egypt and commented about the burial of his body (verse 22). By faith, Moses's parents hid him from the king because they knew he was special and could not be killed as the edict from the king commanded of first born males (verse 23). By faith, Moses led God's people and kept God's decrees (verses 24-28). By faith, Rahab, the prostitute, welcomed spies and was not killed with the disobedient (verse 31). These are only a few examples. Hebrews 11 adds that the world was created by faith (verse 3), the people passed through the Red Sea by faith (verse 29), and the walls of Jericho fell by faith (verse 30).

Verses 32-38 (NIV) read:

"And what more shall I say? I do not have time to tell about Gideon, Barak, Samson and Jephthah, about David and Samuel and the prophets, who through faith conquered kingdoms, gave justice, and gained what was promised those who shut the mouths of lions, quenched the fury of the flames, and escaped the edge of the sword; whose weakness was turned to strength; and who became powerful in battle and routed foreign armies. Women received back their dead, raised to life again. There were others who were tortured, refusing to be released so that they might gain an even better resurrection. Some faced jeers and flogging, and even chains and imprisonment. They were put to death by stoning; they were sawed in two, and they were killed by the sword. They went about in sheepskins and goatskins, destitute, persecuted and mistreated— the world was not worthy of them. They wandered in deserts and mountains, living in caves and in holes in the ground."

Hebrews 11 is a Scripture that proves that walking in faith is not easy. I love that these men and women of the Bible were faithful with what God had placed in their hands, that included running from an enemy, being persecuted for preaching, or suffering on behalf of Jesus's name. These men and women of the Bible exuded faith even among hardship. In fact, the difficulty is what brought each man and woman in Hebrews 11 to place their faith in Him. They were incapable of facing life's challenges on their own and needed to place their faith in someone greater than themselves. Through God, these men and women grew in their faith and finished the races God had set before them. Each man and woman from Hebrews made a decision to be faithful to God by using what God gave them to give Him glory. Therefore, God blessed the men and women of Hebrews 11 because they remained faithful to Him. God's blessings require faithfulness. Blessings are a result of faith because when we place our faith in Him, we are able to experience His mercies that are new every morning. Lamentations 3:22-23 (NIV) says, "The steadfast love of the Lord never ceases; his mercies never come to an end; they are new every morning; great is your faithfulness."

God's blessings require faithfulness.

God gives each of His people personalities, passions, strengths, weaknesses, talents, and skills so that we can give them back to Him. When we give back to God what He has given us, He is able to use us to give His name praise and honor. When we are faithful by giving God even the seemingly small or insignificant aspects of our lives, He blesses us with His faithfulness. Give God everything in your life because the small and insignificant parts are often the most important parts. Be faithful with the blessings God has given to you by giving those blessings back to God and humbly serving Him alone with a faith-filled heart. Like those in the book of Hebrews who were unable to see God's promise fulfilled, we need to live a faithful allegiance to God even if we do not see God's promises in our own lives resolved through immediate fulfillment.

Be faithful with the blessings God has given to you by giving those blessings back to God and humbly serving Him alone with a faith-filled heart.

The people named in Hebrews did not experience the ultimate promise because God had not yet sent His son to save the world from sin. Jesus gives us an even greater reason to persevere through trials and cling to faith. The people listed in Hebrews 11 were great men and women of faith; however, they could not be made "complete" or "perfect." Being made "complete" or "perfect" is only possible with Jesus. These admirable men and women of faith could look forward to Jesus's coming, whereas we look at Jesus's coming from behind and soak in the fruit of His work. The work of Christ is what makes those of the Old Testament, those of the New Testament, and those following Jesus today alike in the presence of God. Thankfully, we have men and women to admire both in the Old Testament and the New Testament who upheld great faith. These examples should inspire, encourage, and motivate us to pursue God with faithfulness because, ultimately, He is the One who has always been faithful to us.

TRUSTING GOD'S FAITHFULNESS

I love the timing of God's words, especially in my moment of panic on the interstate. When God said, "Do not be afraid, I am with you," I had already left CVS and plugged my address into the GPS in my car. Just as a car has its own GPS built within its software, you have access to a God who is the ultimate GPS of everything in life. I realized that I would rather be in my car with God and no GPS than in my car without God and with a GPS. Even though I felt better with my car's GPS, the GPS in my car would only direct me to my house or to any other destination I requested. God as our GPS can guide us anywhere. Through His faithfulness, God can take us many more places than a GPS can, and He positions us better than a GPS can because He is omnipresent. He never fails to be faithful in His guidance. Unlike my car, God never runs low on gas. Unlike my phone, God never dies. Unlike me suffering from the effects of my ear infection, God is never hindered by pain. Because God is who He says He is, He remains faithful. His faithfulness allows us to trust Him and experience His character more fully.

PRAY

God,
Thank You for being faithful to Your Word and Your promises. Help me cling to You because You are consistently present in my life. God, thank You for reminding me of Your truth and displaying its validity in my life daily. Help me realize the vastness of Your faithfulness and guide me to place my trust in You. Amen.

PRAISE

Song: "Goodness of God" by Cece Winans

PAUSE

1. What are ways God has been faithful to you?

2. How can you be a faithful follower of God and trust Him even amidst uncertainty?

3. What are some blessings God has placed in your hands that require you to be faithful?

READ: HEBREWS 11

1. What do these verses reveal about God?

2. What do these verses reveal about you?

3. What do you feel God calling you to do in response to reading these verses?

REMEMBER

The world pursues a life full of fear, but Jesus followers pursue firm belief in God's consistent character through the fruit of faithfulness.

CHAPTER 9

Gentleness

Do you know anyone whom you would describe as gentle? When I think of gentleness, I envision Mrs. Becky, my mom's best friend. When we were little, my sister and I loved to play with Mrs. Becky's daughter, Lydia. Any time Mary Claire and I went to Lydia's house, we played together for hours. We loved to pretend we were fairies, put on gymnastics shows, or make crafts together. Although I remember these memories, I most often remember Mrs. Becky's gentle spirit. I really enjoyed going to her house because she always made me feel like the most special person in the room. When you talked to Mrs. Becky, she listened intently. She gave genuine compliments and always encouraged others. She never failed to make me feel uplifted when I had the privilege of visiting her home. People like Mrs. Becky are ones worth keeping around. Gentle people make a difference because they pursue relationships with true humility. Gentleness is not demanding one's rights, having a superior attitude, or timidity/passiveness. Instead, it is the special quality of meekness. "Gentleness" in Greek is *praotetos*. This expresses an inward grace of the soul and calmness toward God. *Anah* is the Hebrew word for gentleness. This word can also be closely tied to humility. Being teachable and open minded are key components of being gentle. Moderation and a proclivity not to become angry are components of a gentle spirit, which is precious to God according to Scripture. Mrs. Becky is probably one of the most gentle people I have ever met. Any time I have ever told her how much I admire her gentleness, she displays great humility. She always says that everything good in her life comes from God. This aspect of humility continues to inspire me because gentleness does not come from our own abilities. Instead, gentleness grows as a fruit of the Spirit in our lives when we choose to pursue humility in our relationships with others and God.

Please read the verses below carefully to learn more about God's gentleness:

> "But in your hearts honor Christ the Lord as holy, always being prepared to make a defense to anyone who asks you for a reason for the hope that is in you; yet do it with gentleness and respect."
> — 1 Peter 3:15 (ESV)

> "A soft answer turns away wrath, but a harsh word stirs up anger."
> — Proverbs 15:1 (ESV)

> "You have given me the shield of your salvation, and your right hand supported me, and your gentleness made me great."
> — Psalm 18:35 (ESV)

What do the verses above communicate about gentleness?

BABYSITTING

Babysitting is one of the most fun, yet craziest jobs ever! I have learned so much from babysitting over the past few years. I started babysitting as soon as I could drive. I have enjoyed babysitting because it provides wonderful experiences to learn and have fun with kids. Although the families I have interacted with are all very different, I see one consistent theme throughout my babysitting adventures. Whether I am watching a middle school-aged child or a one-year-old, gentleness is always the best way to approach any and every scenario. Gentleness is a wonderful fruit of the Spirit that describes the quality of being kind, tender, or mild-mannered. Gentleness is less talked about, but this does not limit its importance and power. Sadly, we often allow gentleness to slip from our focus because of qualities like frustration, bitterness, pride, and anger. When we allow these qualities to override gentleness, we become more susceptible to an unhappy lifestyle. Unfortunately, gentleness is often forgotten because rather than thinking to respond gently in the Spirit, we respond with negative emotions in the flesh. When emotions like frustration, bitterness, pride, and anger enter our lives, we need to allow gentleness to surpass these qualities. Something God has taught me is that gentleness is not an emotion—it is a fruit of the Spirit. Gentleness is a lost quality because people are quick to react and slow to recognize the Spirit's nudge toward this fruit of the Spirit. People are so easily angered or frustrated by political issues, racial tension, or social media comments that they forget what gentleness looks like. Responding and reacting in gentleness can transform someone's life—including your own. 1 Peter 3:4 (NLT) says, "Rather, it should be that of your inner self, the unfading beauty of a gentle and quiet spirit, which is of great worth in God's sight." There is a unique difference in those who are blessed by the Spirit with gentleness.

AMAZON ALEXA

One of the first families I started consistently babysitting for was a family with triplets. At first, I was intimidated when their mom told me about her children being triplets; however, once I met them, I knew we would have a blast together. All three kids (Connor, Audrey, and Lauren) have amazing personalities, unique talents, and kind hearts. I first met them when they were nine years old, and ever since then, we have shared some amazing memories together. Over the summers, I was with the triplets two or three times a week for about five hours a day. This extended time together allowed me to get to know the triplets very quickly. Thankfully, because it was summer, we were able to swim at their neighborhood pool, go get ice cream, or play games together. The opportunities for fun were endless! For a change, I would sometimes take the triplets to my house. Although both houses were great, my house had an Amazon Alexa. They did not have an Alexa at their house, so when they came to our house, they ran straight to our Alexa. They thought it was so cool that Alexa can play songs, tell jokes, or explain fun facts. My brothers, Noah and Muntu, also love Alexa, so they had a great time teaching the triplets how to use it. Before long, they knew every tip and trick to utilizing all the benefits of the device.

One time when the triplets, my brothers, and I were downstairs at my house, Lauren needed something from upstairs, so I decided to go with her while the others continued to play downstairs. Lauren and I were gone for about a minute, but when I came back downstairs, I could tell it had been a disastrous sixty seconds. As I rounded the corner to go downstairs, I heard Connor crying loudly on our couch.

My initial thought was that my brothers were being too rough and accidentally hurt Connor while playing. However, I found out from the others downstairs that Connor was on the floor by the couch hiding from my brothers when our Amazon Alexa fell from the couch and hit Connor in the mouth. Initially, I was confused as to how Alexa fell onto Connor's mouth—it sounded absurd in the moment, and it still sounds absurd as I replay the story inside my head! I did not have time to dissect all the details of the chaotic story because when everyone else downstairs was trying to explain to me what happened, I was swarmed with worry. As I looked at Connor, my heart dropped because his smile was missing part of his front tooth! When our Alexa fell, Connor's mouth must have been open, because half of Connor's front tooth was chipped! I was shocked at this moment because Connor was in pain, Lauren started crying out of concern for her brother, Audrey was holding up the part of Connor's front tooth that had been chipped seconds before, and my brothers were standing next to me with wide-eyed expressions. I tried my best to calm everyone down, but I could barely calm myself down. This was crazy!

I assumed that the chaos of this incident meant that it was time for the triplets to go home; however, I had no idea how their parents would react now that Connor was missing half his tooth. The story sounds absurd; however, I knew the right thing to do was explain honestly and apologize sincerely. Because the triplets' mom did not expect them to be home for another hour or two, I nervously texted her a summary of what had happened and decided to drive them home so Connor could receive the help he needed to fix his mouth. The triplets' mom was very kind in her response to me via text, so I was hopeful that everything would be okay when I took the kids home. Thankfully, she was so gracious and gentle to me when she heard the full story of what happened. I was amazed that she was not upset with me at all. I thought I might lose a babysitting job, but she was so understanding. She took Connor to the dentist the next day and thankfully, they scheduled an appointment to fix his tooth. A few days later, Connor had a new smile that looked as radiant as the one before. I was so glad that the triplets' parents treated me so gently. I was more amazed when I realized I did not deserve to be treated this way. I was responsible for Connor while he was at my house, so it was partially my fault that Connor's tooth was chipped by our Amazon Alexa. They had every right to be upset with me, but they weren't at all! Their mom and dad told me not to worry one bit and they would take care of everything. They knew that the dentist could fix the tooth and that Connor would be perfectly fine. This is how God speaks to us because He gently reminds us that we do not need to worry. God gently restores us from worrying to trusting in Him. Living life worrying is debilitating, but living life trusting is refreshing. Even when your circumstances look as chaotic as my babysitting experience, God will be gentle in the way He responds to you. This is such a wonderful reminder for you and me. Our sins, disobedience, guilt, or shame cannot stand in the way of God's gentleness. God punishes when necessary because He is a just God; however, He embraces His children with gentleness and discipline because He deeply cares. Nothing we do or do not do can prohibit us from experiencing God's gentleness. Instead, the weak and broken parts in our lives should help us recognize our deep need for God's gentle relationship with us. Do not be scared as you approach God like I was when I approached the triplets' parents. Instead, be honest about your circumstances, admit your mistakes, and allow God to pursue you with His transformative and merciful gentleness.

> *Living life worrying is debilitating, but living life trusting is refreshing.*

LIGHTS OUT

Another babysitting story that reminds me of gentleness is when I was babysitting with a friend for a few families while the parents had Bible study. All the kids, my friend, and I played in the basement while the parents had Bible study upstairs. The family who hosted this Bible study has an amazing space for playing. Their basement is filled with a ninja warrior course, a TV, thousands of Legos, books, and other fun toys as well. Everything was going smoothly until all of a sudden, the power went out. It did not take long for every single kid in the room to scream. No one could see anything, including me because every light in the basement went out and there weren't many windows. I grabbed my phone, and my friend used her phone, but there wasn't nearly enough light to shine throughout the entire basement. Thankfully, the parents must have heard the chaos from upstairs and they were able to have the lights back on in no time. I noticed that the youngest little boy was still crying even after the lights were turned on. As I was on my way over to comfort him, his dad came running down the stairs. The boy's dad heard his cry and arrived to pick him up before I could. Just as the boy's dad came running to him to comfort him, God runs toward us ready to comfort us, too. The boy's dad was on the move to find his son because he heard him crying. Similarly, God hears our cries and is always the first to offer us His comfort. God is always there to carry us when we need Him most.

I am in awe of how the little boy's dad heard him crying because there were many other kids playing loudly. We had a movie playing on the TV, some kids were loudly digging through a big pile of Legos, and others were playing on the ninja warrior course. However, despite all of the commotion, the little boy's dad came running from upstairs and met his child in the basement. The father scooped his boy into his arms and quieted his crying. The little boy stopped crying as soon as he felt his dad's gentle touch. Once the little boy realized that he was safe in his dad's arms, he felt better. Just as the little boy's dad heard him crying and came down the stairs quickly to comfort him, God hears our cries and prayers and runs to us, ready to gently embrace us in His arms. Just as the little boy's dad traveled from the upstairs level of the home to the basement, God will travel any height or distance to meet you where you are. I can assure you that God is willing to go much further than the distance between the main level of the home and the basement to comfort you. Just as the little boy's dad held him after the power came back on, God gently holds us as we transition from the darkness to His divine light. The light of the Lord gives us confidence and trust. When we run from God, He responds to us, gently begging us to come back to Him. When we hide from God, He is already in our hiding spot gently waiting to comfort us in His love. When we are pushed away from God, He has already prepared to lift us back up gently into the palm of His secure hand. Jesus is gentle; He always has been, and He always will be.

> *Jesus is gentle; He always has been, and He always will be.*

THE SHEPHERD AND THE SHEEP

One of my favorite passages in the Bible is John 10 because it talks about the gentleness of God using the example of sheep and a shepherd. John 10:14-18 (NLT) says, "I am the good shepherd; I know my sheep and my sheep know me— just as the Father knows me and I know the Father—and I lay down my life for the sheep. I have other sheep that are not of this sheep pen. I must bring them also. They too will listen to my voice, and there shall be one flock and one shepherd. The reason my Father loves me is that I lay down my life—only to take it up again. No one takes it from me, but I lay it down of my own accord. I have the authority to lay it down and the authority to take it up again. This command I received from my Father." Like the baby's dad, Jesus sees us and hears our cries. Jesus views His people as sheep because they are incapable on their own. However, with Jesus, a sheep can recognize a familiar voice and follow its guidance just as the baby's dad heard his little boy crying and came running to him. Like the boy's dad used his voice to comfort his son, Jesus uses his voice to gently direct and instruct us.

To fully understand gentleness, we need to study the life of Jesus. We often feel that in order to communicate our thoughts, opinions, and beliefs, we must do so in a strong and oftentimes aggressive way, but did Jesus respond or act this way? Absolutely not! When people hurt Jesus, He always responded with careful words and actions. Genuine gentleness begins with the true source, which is Jesus Himself. When you are struggling to be gentle with your words or actions, trust Jesus and ask Him for help. Give the Holy Spirit permission to work in your heart and produce gentleness rather than a hot-tempered or easily angered spirit. Remember that Jesus's gentleness is a precious gift because it flows from the abundance of His perfect character.

GENTLENESS AND HUMILITY

One of the sweetest ways to express gentleness is through humility. Oftentimes, the words "gentleness" and "humility" are interchangeable. These words have a close tie to one another because both involve recognizing that God is superior in all things. I had to humble myself in both babysitting experiences. Gentleness requires a level of humility. When God softens our hearts to make us more gentle, He grows humility in us. Together, gentleness and humility help us recognize the people God puts around us and gives us the ability to treat them well. Some of the most gentle and humble people I know are great at interacting with others and responding to certain situations—especially difficult or frustrating ones. For example, the triplets' parents weren't mad at me for what had happened to Connor at my house. Instead, their mom chose to respond to the chaotic situation with gentleness and humility. This calmed the environment and immensely helped me as I apologized to them and processed the situation.

> *Gentleness requires a level of humility.*

Additionally, when the lights went out in the basement as I was babysitting, the little boy's dad ran over to him with a gentle touch. The gentleness he provided came from a humble position as he left his Bible study upstairs and came running downstairs to comfort his son. This is exactly what Jesus did for us. He came down from heaven to earth to serve as our Shepherd. As a shepherd, He treated His people gently and with great humility. Jesus continues to treat us gently as He guides us, forgives us, and loves us. Jesus's gentleness and humility are truly the best testament to living a life honoring to God.

PRAY

Dear Jesus,
Gentleness is difficult, especially since it is not of immense value to most people today. Help me remember that gentleness is of value to You and can be used to greatly impact the Kingdom of God. Guide me to speak, act, and think gently through humility so that I may reflect Christ more fully. Help me to be gentle even when emotions of frustration, jealousy, or anger arise. Grant me a gentle and quiet spirit that is deemed precious in Your sight. Amen.

PRAISE

Song: "Gentle Jesus" by Matt and Josie Minikus

PAUSE

1. Do you know anyone who has the gift of gentleness?

2. What are ways you can embrace gentleness even when culture strays away from it?

3. How can you make practical changes to your lifestyle to embody gentleness and humility?

READ: JOHN 10:1-21

1. What do these verses reveal about God?

2. What do these verses reveal about you?

3. What do you feel God calling you to do in response to reading these verses?

REMEMBER

The world pursues prideful attitudes, but Jesus followers pursue a posture of shepherding others through the fruit of gentleness.

CHAPTER 10

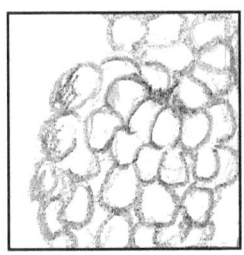

Self-Control

Let's be honest with one another. Most of us do not hear the words "self control" and jump with excitement. Many times, self-control is considered one of the hardest fruits of the Spirit to develop. Why is self-control so difficult at times? Self-control is challenging for individuals for various reasons; however, one common struggle stems from the way our culture operates. For instance, many people support the messages of accumulating more even when God has given us enough, giving less even though God commands us to share, or working harder to build a name for ourselves when God explains that we are to glorify Him. The culture preaches the opposite message of the Bible, so oftentimes, as Christians, we feel confused. Which way do we turn? How do we choose to live? Do we follow the world's ways or do we choose self-control in order to step further into God's plans? These are questions we need to ask ourselves and consider. Many believe that choosing self-control is not worth it because we lose freedom. However, the Bible argues just the opposite. When we choose self-control rather than self-seeking behavior, we experience biblical freedom God promises to us in Scripture. Self-control leads us to diligently work, encourage others, and focus on God. Self-control works on behalf of others. It includes self-discipline and denial of the self to adhere to God's work through the Spirit. This word in Greek is *ekrategias*. This means that self-control consists of sufficiency and contentment. The word in Hebrew is *engkratea*, which means inner strength. This describes strength in turning away from the evil desires of the world. God is the source of inner strength. Although the world may not encourage self-control as the

Bible does, let's jump into Scripture together to see how pursuing self-control can lead us toward true freedom in Christ.

Read the verses below to learn more about self-control in Scripture:

"For God gave us a spirit, not of fear but power and love and self-control." — 2 Timothy 1:7 (ESV)

"A man without self-control is like a city broken into and left without walls." — Proverbs 25:28 (ESV)

"For you were called to freedom, brothers. Only do not use your freedom as an opportunity for the flesh, but through love serve one another." — Galatians 5:13 (ESV)

What do the verses above communicate about self-control?

MY BUTTERFLY BIRTHDAY PARTY

Some of my favorite memories consist of celebrating birthdays. All birthdays are significant, but thirteenth birthdays are especially important because they mark the transition from childhood to adolescence. Because my parents wanted to celebrate this exciting transition with me, they planned a wonderful, butterfly-themed party when I turned thirteen. One memory I will never forget was when my parents shared with me the surprising news that they ordered real butterflies to be released at my party. At first, I was slightly confused because I had no idea you could order butterflies. The butterflies were sent to my house and in order to protect them, they arrived individually wrapped and frozen. The fact that someone could order butterflies wasn't nearly as shocking as hearing that they were delivered frozen! I am still not sure how the butterflies stayed alive even though they were frozen, but every butterfly was beautiful, and my friends and I were able to release them into the sky at my birthday party. My mom had my friends and I carefully line up in a row to release the butterflies. The twelve friends at my party and I were so excited because this was the moment we had been waiting for! As we prepared to release our butterflies, we decided to stand on the edge of our dock facing our pond. We unwrapped our butterflies and on the count of three, we released them into the blue sky. They were so beautiful as they flew in different directions across the water. We admired their intricate designs and bright colors as they gracefully fluttered in the air. Releasing butterflies was by far one of the best activities I had ever participated in at a birthday party!

As I reflect on my thirteenth birthday party, I find it interesting that butterflies symbolize transition. One of the most beautiful examples of transition in God's creation is the way a caterpillar transforms into a butterfly. This reminds me of how children grow to become teenagers. As the butterflies flew away on my birthday, it reminded me that a butterfly has much more freedom when it grows wings because it is no longer restricted to its structure as a caterpillar. A butterfly can use its wings to fly to its preferred destination. However, a caterpillar can only travel so far because of its natural shape and structure. Caterpillars travel less distance in a slower time frame. They maneuver themselves on the ground whereas butterflies travel more distance because they can fly in the sky at a much greater speed. Teenagers participate in more activities whereas children are limited due to their maturity level and age. Just as butterflies have more freedom than caterpillars, teenagers have more freedom than children. During transitions like becoming a teenager, I have found that I need more self-control from the Lord. When changes occur, what once was stable is now different. Therefore, I have needed to strongly implement self-control during transitional seasons of my life. Having self-control is important for navigating new opportunities and emerging freedoms.

One form of freedom many teenagers enjoy is owning a cell phone, with many kids receiving their first phone before age thirteen. Having a phone for the first time is an exciting experience. I was thirteen years old when my parents gave me my first phone. After the amazing butterfly release experience, my friends and family were gathered in my living room, and I began opening birthday presents. As I was opening gifts, a strange, fairy-like noise began to fill the room. At first, it was barely noticeable because it was so quiet; however, it grew louder and louder. Finally, I realized the fairy-like noise was a ringtone sounding from the new iPhone 6 my parents had bought for me. My mom and dad chose to surprise me by hiding the phone in the crevice of the couch I was sitting on. When I pulled out the phone from the couch cushion, my first thought was, "Wait, now I have to answer phone calls." I find it funny that this was my first thought as a thirteen-year-old receiving my new phone. I didn't initially think, "Now I can text my friends" or "I can play games" or "I can take pictures." Although I was excited to receive my phone, I also realized the implications of owning one. I had come to the realization that phones bring about a whole new kind of freedom. I had seen my parents answer the phone multiple times and I had even answered their phones for them on a few occasions; however, it was officially my turn now. Sixth-grade me felt excited, but also nervous because having a phone of my own was a freedom I had never experienced before. The opportunities that arise through our phones' technologies are endless. Freedom within the technological world is practically unescapable. Receiving a phone on my thirteenth birthday heightened my awareness of the new freedoms I could experience. I also began to learn that with new freedoms also comes the need for greater levels of self-control.

THE GIFT OF FREEDOM

Freedom is a gift that we are responsible for stewarding. When any amount of freedom is offered to us, we must ask God for self-control. Just like it sounds, self-control is the ability to control oneself, in particular one's emotions and desires, or the expression of them in one's behavior, especially in difficult situations. For example, phones offer vast amounts of freedom; therefore, large amounts of self-control are necessary to help us best handle freedoms in the technological world. The more freedom God blesses us with, the more self-control we need to use. Just like when someone receives a phone for the first time, the butterfly experiences many freedoms all at once too. Once the caterpillar transforms into a butterfly, the butterfly's wings can transport the butterfly from one area to the next. Butterflies can see the world at a much faster rate once they are equipped to fly. Similarly, teenagers experience the same flow of freedom when using a phone for the first time. Once a phone is placed in someone's hands, they have access to everything in the technological world because of the seemingly infinite abilities of devices. With these newfound freedoms, the fruit of the Spirit called self-control is essential.

> *When any amount of freedom is offered to us, we must ask God for self-control.*

Freedom is a beautiful blessing when used in ways that honor God. The first step to using self-control to harness our freedoms in God-honoring ways is calling on God for guidance. Asking for the Lord's help is always the best and first step to take. He

> *Asking for the Lord's help is always the best and first step to take.*

will never lead you in the wrong direction and He will always provide exactly what you need. Additionally, a lesson I have learned is that no matter who you are, how old you are, or what you like to do, you will always need help and guidance from the Lord, but also from those who are older and wiser. For example, when a teenager first receives a phone, self-control is immediately challenged due to overwhelming and new freedoms. However, older adults who may have several years of experience with a phone can better equip younger teenagers on how to effectively manage this newfound freedom through self-control. For example, I learned a healthy habit from my parents. They suggested I charge my phone downstairs at night so that my phone was away from my bedroom. Charging my phone downstairs forces me to unplug both at night and in the mornings. This benefited my quiet times with the Lord in a very impactful way because I was able to end my day with the Lord on my mind (rather than checking my phone one last time) and I was able to begin my day with my daily prayer and devotion (without my phone being a distraction). This habit is one I started a few years ago and I still use it today because it has benefited me immensely. I was hesitant at first because this idea of charging my phone elsewhere was new to me. However, it made such a positive difference, and I am thankful for my parents' advice. When I am at my house, on vacation, or visiting a new place, I always try to charge my phone further away from me so I can have some special time to unwind and recharge.

SELF-CONTROL EXPRESSED THROUGH FREEDOM

People crave freedom, but to successfully live in freedom, self-control must be a priority. Self-control is one of the fruits of the Spirit that takes dedication to develop; however, the time, effort, and energy you spend committing to controlling your emotions and desires will promise benefits in this life and the life to come. For example, if self-control consists of controlling your emotions and desires, think about what would happen without self-control. When I turned thirteen, I experienced the new freedom of having a phone and I had to practice self-control as I learned to effectively use my phone. However, if I did not practice controlling my emotions or desires, I would not be able to enjoy the freedom of having a phone. Self-control isn't our natural choice, but it leads us to control freedoms in ways that allow us to live abundantly. Titus 2:11-12 (NIV) says, "For the grace of God has appeared that offers salvation to all people. It teaches us to say 'No' to ungodliness and worldly passions, and to live self-controlled, upright, and godly lives in this present age…" Self-control may seem like a restriction; however, living an upright and godly life opens opportunities for God to use His people. When we pursue self-control, God is able to use our circumstances for our good and His glory.

> *When we pursue self-control, God is able to use our circumstances for our good and His glory.*

Even though I have only had my phone for ten years, I have seen the difference when I choose to practice self-control and when I decide to disregard it. For instance, when I decide to read, study, or do homework, having my phone away from me helps me complete my work much faster. When I am with friends, I find that the time we have together is maximized when we engage with each other face-to-face rather than communicating via a screen. Instead of having my phone with me all the time, I find that it is much nicer to unplug.

Self-control is needed when approaching technology; however, it is also needed in every other area of your life. For example, if you desire to play basketball, you must control your desire to practice and prepare for competitions. If you would like to eat healthier, you must control your habits and internal desires by remembering what foods are best for you. If you are angry with a friend because they lied to you, to handle this situation the right way, you must display Christ-like qualities to the other person rather than lashing out to him/her about why you are upset. Self-control may seem to be a quality that restricts freedoms because it causes you to be self-aware; however, the ability to control emotions and desires leads you to newfound freedoms within every opportunity.

Self-control is life-changing if you are willing to put it into practice. This valuable quality has allowed me to use my time more effectively because I am better focused on the specific task at hand. I have learned to use self-control to restrict time on my phone, to enhance the time I spend with others, and to handle difficult situations in an appropriate and godly way. When you follow through with self-control and truly commit to investment in this quality, you will see tremendous results and eternal blessings. Most importantly, you can rest in the knowledge that you are like a butterfly, beautiful and free. God has blessed you with various freedoms and I encourage you to fully embrace those freedoms and cultivate them well by practicing self-control.

PRAY

Everlasting Father,
Thank You for giving us a spirit of power, love, and self-control. Guide me to use self-control as I navigate the freedoms You bless me with. Help me to realize that the freedom I have in Christ is a gift I am responsible for stewarding. Lead me to self-control even when it is difficult to choose that path. Initially, self-control is not always the most appealing option; however, remind me that self-control makes me more like You and guides me to understand more of Your character and Kingdom. Amen.

PRAISE

Song: "Free, Amen" by We The Kingdom

PAUSE

1. What freedoms do you desire? Why?

2. Do you feel like your freedoms have helped you grow closer to the Lord?

3. In what areas of life do you need to implement self-control?

READ: ROMANS 6:15-23

1. What do these verses reveal about God?

2. What do these verses reveal about you?

3. What do you feel God calling you to do in response to reading these verses?

REMEMBER

The world pursues freedom irresponsibly, but Jesus followers pursue freedom wisely through the fruit of self-control.

CHAPTER 11
Fruit Nourishes Us

Now that we have explored all nine of the fruit of the Spirit, let's recap what we have learned so far. Although each of the fruits of the Spirit are different from one another, they all point to God's character. These qualities are not ones we produce on our own; however, they are ones that God cultivates in and through us. The fruit of the Spirit give us the opportunity to walk away from the flesh and our sinful desires. Instead, we walk with the Spirit in the new life He has provided for us. The ways of the flesh and the way of the Spirit are separate. Half of our lives can not be devoted to the Spirit while the other half is devoted to the flesh. We must surrender everything to the Holy Spirit. Walking in His ways requires us to obey the Word of God, which says that we have been called to bear fruit. In Ephesians 4:1, Paul says that we are to live life worthy of our calling. John 15 reminds us that our calling is to bear fruit. When Jesus was preparing His disciples for His death, He commanded that they bear fruit. This is not a recommendation from Jesus; it is a command. Bearing fruit is also more than a command from Jesus in Scripture. Bearing fruit is also our purpose—we are to glorify God by bearing fruit that testifies to His great name and beautiful character.

HERE IS A REMINDER THAT THE SPIRIT'S F.R.U.I.T. NOURISHES THE HEART AND MIND:

FLOURISHES by walking with the Holy Spirit:

"So I say, walk by the Spirit, and you will not gratify the desires of the flesh. For the flesh desires what is contrary to the Spirit, and the Spirit what is contrary to the flesh. They are in conflict with each other, so that you are not to do whatever you want. But if you are led by the Spirit, you are not under the law." — Galatians 5:16-18 (NIV)

It is so important for us to remember that the fruit of the Spirit flourish in our lives when we are walking with the Holy Spirit. Letting the Holy Spirit lead you in every part of your life is difficult because it requires surrender, but this is a step worth taking. The verses in Galatians 5:16-18 help us understand that when we walk with the Spirit and surrender to Him, we are fulfilling the Spirit's desires rather than fleshly desires. Being led by the Spirit also indicates that we are not under the law, but instead, we are given an opportunity for freedom through the Holy Spirit. In order for the fruit of the Spirit to flourish in our lives, we must always remember that fruit is cultivated from the Holy Spirit's power—not our own. We need to ask the Holy Spirit to help us surrender the desires of our flesh so that we can obey the promptings of the Spirit. Spend time walking with the Spirit because in doing so, the fruit of the Spirit will begin to flourish in your life. Also, your fleshly desires will begin to transform into desires that align with God and His will for your life. Walking with the Spirit changes everything as it helps us rely on God's transformative work in our hearts and minds.

ROOTED in the life of Christ:

"Those who belong to Christ Jesus have crucified the flesh with its passions and desires." — Galatians 5:24 (NIV)

The fruit of the Spirit is rooted in the life of Christ. Throughout the entire Old Testament, Jesus's time on earth was predicted. The New Testament outlines Jesus's life more specifically and provides details of Jesus' character. Jesus's qualities are numerous, but they can be summarized using the nine fruits of the Spirit. In Galatians 5:24, Paul writes that those who belong to Christ are ones who are crucified with the flesh and its passion and desires. Paul is emphasizing that crucifying the flesh means dying as Christ did. In other words, we must leave the old self and live within the new life Jesus died to give us. When Jesus was crucified, the Roman citizens hung his body on a cross, which was fulfilling God's intended plan. God prepared Jesus to be crucified to redeem His people. Therefore, when Paul uses the word "crucified" in Galatians, it is important because in order to be filled with the fruit of the Spirit, we need to crucify the flesh's passions and desires. When we surrender ourselves in this way to the Spirit, our lives become rooted in the life of Christ, and we are ready to embrace the fruit of the Spirit. Just as Christ surrendered Himself on behalf of all sinners, we need to give ourselves to the Spirit and let Him work in and through us to give God glory.

UNDERSTOOD through freedom:

"You, my brothers and sisters, were called to be free. But do not use your freedom to indulge the flesh; rather, serve one another humbly in love. For the entire law is fulfilled in keeping this one command: "Love your neighbor as yourself." — Galatians 5:13-14 (NIV)

One important aspect of the fruit of the Spirit is the way it is understood through freedom in Christ. In Galatians 5:13-14, Paul says that God's people are called to be free. It is crucial to remember that Paul's words in Galatians were surprising to the initial readers of this letter because although Paul's words aligned with the Bible, they did not match the Galatian churches' false teachings about the gospel. Most people would not associate the law with freedom because the law served as a way to keep the Israelites obedient to God. However, because Christ died and resurrected, we no longer have responsibility to fully obey the law. In fact, because of our sinful nature, we are unable to fully obey the law. In Jesus's name, we are set free because Christ died the death we were supposed to die and lived the righteous life we could never live. The law is still valuable because it helps us honor God and become like Him. However, the law does not keep us in bondage. In fact, it does the exact opposite. The law gives us freedom in Christ to serve one another in love rather than indulge in the flesh. This means that we have the opportunity to live for someone/something greater than ourselves. When we live in love, we live in the Spirit. Instead of allowing our flesh to control us, freedom in Christ gives the Spirit power to control us. This means that when the Spirit rules over our lives, we can grow in the fruit of the Spirit and learn how to live in the freedoms Christ gives to us through His death on the cross. Remembering the source of freedom allows us to reflect on God and understand His character more fully. Then, as we understand God's character better, He will unveil Himself to us personally and plant the fruit of the Spirit in our lives.

ILLUMINATES the guidance of God:

> "Since we live by the Spirit, let us keep in step with the Spirit. Let us not become conceited, provoking and envying each other."
> — Galatians 5:25-26 (NIV)

Another beautiful part of the fruit of the Spirit is the way it points us to God and His guidance. Keeping in step with the Spirit allows us to walk with God and learn the plans He has for us. In Galatians 5:25-26, Paul says that those who live in the Spirit must keep in step with the Spirit. This means that in order to live in the Spirit, your life must consistently produce the fruit of the Spirit. This does not mean that your life has to be perfect, and you have to fully embody every quality of Christ correctly. Instead, this means that you must actively seek the Spirit and His guidance. When you seek the Spirit by keeping in step with Him, you read His Word, pray to Him, and praise His name. As you desire the Holy Spirit's guidance, the fruit of the Spirit will naturally grow in your life. Rather than becoming conceited, provoking, or envying someone, the Spirit kills those fleshly desires by guiding us to pursue Christ and His ways instead. The Holy Spirit illuminates the path of growth by guiding us to display the fruit of the Spirit.

TEACHES biblically within the Kingdom:

> "The acts of the flesh are obvious: sexual immorality, impurity and debauchery; idolatry and witchcraft; hatred, discord, jealousy, fits of rage, selfish ambition, dissensions, factions and envy; drunkenness, orgies, and the like. I warn you, as I did before, that those who live like this will not inherit the kingdom of God." — Galatians 5:19-21 (NIV)

The fruit of the Spirit teaches truth that aligns beautifully with the rest of the Scriptures in the Bible. In Galatians 5:19-21, the acts of the flesh are stated as obvious. Paul describes fleshly desires as "obvious" to show they clearly do not align with the Bible. Therefore, they are obviously noticeable as fleshly desires because they do not correlate with Christ's character. Those who live according to the flesh will not inherit the Kingdom of God. However, those who adhere to the Spirit inherit the Kingdom of God because they seek the Lord and the fruit of the Spirit in their lives daily. When you ensure that you are aligning yourself with Biblical truth and strength from the Spirit, you will not have to worry about fleshly desires. Instead, you can be confident that you will inherit the Kingdom of God because of Christ's work for you and the Spirit's work in you. God has created a Kingdom family, and He desperately wants you to be a part of it. He is preparing a place for you; therefore, seek Him through His Word and prayer so that you will be equipped to serve within the Kingdom of God.

Let's recap together so we can reflect on what we have learned thus far throughout this study. John 15 is a famous passage known for its discussion about fruit. John 15:5-8 (NIV) says, "I am the vine; you are the branches. If you remain in me and I in you, you will bear much fruit; apart from me you can do nothing. If you do not remain in me, you are like a branch that is thrown away and withers; such branches are picked up, thrown into the fire and burned. If you remain in me and my words remain in you, ask whatever you wish, and it will be done for you. This is to my Father's glory, that you bear much fruit, showing yourselves to be my disciples." This passage highlights the benefits of fruit as well as the dangers of not bearing God's fruit. Jesus states that bearing good fruit stems from remaining in Christ. Jesus says that apart from God we can't do anything, which means that the healthy fruit we bear is not our own. Instead, we must never forget that godly fruit comes from the Lord and His work within us. When we choose not to remain in Him, we are choosing sin. This results in unhealthy fruit growing in our lives. These are the branches that Jesus says will be thrown away: withered, picked up, thrown into the fire, and burned. However, Jesus also writes that when we choose to refrain from sin and remain in Christ, we bear fruit that is pleasing to God. Remaining within the foundation of God's truth is crucial to bearing godly fruit. When we bear fruit, we are doing so for God's glory. Jesus says to His people in John 15 that we are His disciples if we remain in Him. He also says that anything we ask for will be given to us. This does not mean that I could ask for a beach house and God would give me one. However, it does mean that if I ask Him to produce godly fruit in my life, He will gladly cultivate growth in my heart. When we remain in Him, our desires become God's desires. Although there is not anything inherently wrong with wanting a beach house, desire for godly fruit becomes greater when we remain in Him. We will see glimpses of the beauty and power within the fruit of the Spirit. My hope and prayer is that we will see more of God and desire more of His presence in our lives by studying the fruit of the Spirit. May God teach us more about Himself and equip us to bear godly fruit that will outlive us and make a Kingdom impact.

CHAPTER 12

Keep Pressing

I had the great privilege of traveling to Israel in 2023. During our trip, I was able to see many of the places Jesus had been during His time on earth. It was a trip of a lifetime, and if you ever have the chance to visit Israel, you should highly consider going! Being in Israel helped me understand the Bible on a much deeper level. Scriptures I knew became easier to understand as I was able to learn their context and location. Additionally, even familiar passages of Scripture became clearer to me as I was able to gain new perspectives and insights from pastors and guides on our trip. One of my favorite stops on our visit to Israel was our last destination. Before we traveled home, we were able to see the Garden of Gethsemane. It was here where Jesus prayed to the Father His famous words, "Yet not as I will, but what you will" (Matthew 26:39 NIV). It was in the Garden of Gethsemane where Jesus was sweating drops of blood and felt overwhelmed to the point of death (Matthew 26:38). Jesus was burdened by carrying the past, present, and future sin of mankind. Although He was innocent, Jesus submitted to the Father's ways and willingly chose death. We see through the resurrection of Jesus that He chose death so that we could be given new life. This new life Jesus provides us is a life of abiding in Him. Being in the Garden of Gethsemane was an amazing experience because I was able to picture Jesus praying to the Father, interceding on behalf of His people.

In the Garden of Gethsemane, there were many beautiful olive trees surrounding the area. I learned on this trip that olive trees were very valuable in Israel's culture, especially because the olives provided oil and served as food for the people. In order to create olive oil, the people of Israel pressed the olives so that all the valuable oil was extracted. Olive oil was used primarily for cooking, lighting lamps, and anointing for priests and kings. Oftentimes, olive oil was used for cosmetics, medications, soaps, and even currency. Olive oil was a sign of prosperity, joy, and health. Olive oil was a huge resource in ancient Israel, but it is also still used commonly today.

The pressing of olives for olive oil is a beautiful parallel to the life of Jesus and the lives of His followers. Jesus's body was crucified so that His blood could become the atoning sacrifice for all sins—past, present, and future. Jesus experienced pressing. One definition of pressing states, "to apply pressure to something to flatten, shape, or smooth it." Although Jesus's body was not literally pressed, His purpose through the crucifixion is to bring new life to His people. Jesus was pressed, so much so that He was overwhelmed to the point of death. As I have shared with you so far in this study, there are times that I have been overwhelmed, but every time I read about Jesus praying in the Garden of Gethsemane my mind can not even begin to imagine what His thoughts were as He faced dying on the cross. Jesus was overwhelmed to the point of death. Think about that for a moment. He experienced pressing as His disciples failed to believe Him. Jesus experienced pressing as the crowds criticized Him for claiming His own, true identity as the Son of God. Jesus's pressing is also evident through Scripture as He was set on trial, beaten, and insulted before His crucifixion. Just as Jesus was pressed in His days on earth, you and I will be pressed. Sometimes, the fruit we bear is pressed so that the nutrients and resources from it are maximized. While pressing is difficult, it is necessary if we desire to follow Jesus. Pressing is a part of the journey. Just like olive trees yield olive oil, God can use you and me to yield powerful resources to enrich the lives of those around us. Pressing can be uncomfortable, but it is not unbearable. We must remember why God designed pressing. The process of pressing is to bring out the best. God desires to bring value to our lives, but in order to experience this, we must abide, bear fruit, and be willing to endure pressing. Remember the olive trees. They are beautiful and bear healthy fruit. The olives are picked and pressed so that the oil can be used in many different ways by the community. God desires to press you so that His presence and your God-given gifts can bless your community, too.

John 15 reveals that our journeys with the fruit of the Spirit never end because God is always pruning and purifying our hearts. One definition of fruit is "result or reward of work or activity," therefore, bearing the fruit of the Spirit is a continuous effort because our lives of work and activity exist to honor God both on earth and in heaven. Bearing fruit will always be a part of our lives because our goal is to bear fruit through the Spirit's help to learn about God and give His name praise. Our reward is God Himself. Therefore, instilling the fruit of the Spirit in our lives on a daily level is of utmost importance. I love how in Scripture Paul states, "against these things [the fruit of the Spirit] there is no law" (Galatians 5:23). It is so important that we remember this truth. This means that if we cultivate the qualities of love, joy, peace, patience, kindness, goodness, faithfulness, gentleness, and self-control in our lives, we will be living as God called us to live. Therefore, let's strive to be like Jesus through the fruit of the Spirit. When we fail to live according to the fruit of the Spirit, let's ask for God's forgiveness and seek the Spirit's guidance as to how to move forward in a mature, Christ-like way.

Remember the life-changing truths contained in the fruit of the Spirit and ask the Holy Spirit to transform you every day. Utilize these qualities to challenge yourself in your faith and in your relationship with God on a daily level. Thinking about the fruit of the Spirit and living out these characteristics daily is crucial because we are nourished by the Spirit's work in us when we consistently pursue Him. I have challenged myself with the fruit of the Spirit, and it is amazing because there are endless ways to grow in Christ and learn His truth. The fruit of the Spirit are gifts that continue to give to both you and others around you. I challenge you to memorize Galatians 5:22-23 so that those words will be ingrained in your heart forever. There are beautiful truths in God's Word and when you know it for yourself, that is a gift that can never be taken from you. Continue exploring the fruit of the Spirit and please do not let your journey end here. Keep growing through God's provision, Christ's power, and the Holy Spirit's presence.

A BLESSING FOR YOU:

May God give you a deeper understanding of Himself every day. May you continue to grow in awe of His beautiful character. Seek Him all the days of your life. Let Him show you how wonderful He is. May God continue to display His fruit of the Spirit so that you may receive it and share it with those you encounter. May you be abundantly fruitful in godliness so that the fruit produced from within you makes an impact in the present and influences the Kingdom of God in the future. May love, joy, peace, patience, kindness, goodness, faithfulness, gentleness, and self-control fill your life and overflow. May you experience the life God designed for His children—a life of abiding in His presence. May you trust in the Father as the Gardener, cling to Jesus as the Vine, and obey the Holy Spirit as He produces fruit in your life. May you never forget that God has plans for you that no eye has seen, no ear has heard, and no mind has imagined. Live a life of stillness and slowness that you may see, hear, and experience God's powerful, mighty hand working on your behalf. He is for you. He cares so deeply about you. He will use your life as a bright light in our dark world. God never fails and He won't start with you. Believe in God's Word and never let it go. May God give you the courage to keep pressing forward when times are challenging. May you remember that your strength and ability come from Him alone. Never forget that every good and perfect gift comes from our Heavenly Father. He is eager and capable to bear the fruit of the Spirit in and through your life. May people witness your demeanor and notice how beautifully it reflects Jesus. Don't wait another moment—start the Fruit Pursuit now!

Endnotes

[1] Comer, John Mark. *Practicing the Way*. Colorado Springs, WaterBrook, January 16, 2024. 38

[2] Wilkinson, Bruce. *Secrets of the Vine*. Colorado Springs, Multnomah, January 1, 2001. 20 21 103

[3] Moore, Beth. *Chasing Vines*. Carol Stream, Tyndale Momentum, February 4, 2020. 48 72

[4] Wilkinson, Bruce. *Secrets of the Vine*.

All My Thanks...

First, I must thank the Lord for His direction and provision in this project. The Lord's work in my life has been the inspiration for this book. It is only through His guidance and strength that I was equipped to start and complete "Fruit Pursuit." This book was created from God and is for God. May He receive all the glory!

Mom and Dad – Thank you for always supporting me. I appreciate the ways you two have always believed in me. More importantly, you have always believed in what God could do in and through my life. Thank you for providing your valuable insight and wisdom throughout the book writing process. Also, thank you for displaying the fruit of the Spirit in your lives. I will always admire and learn from the fruit God continues to abundantly produce in and through you both.

Christie Carey – Thank you for everything you have done to beautifully create this book. You have a wonderful talent for designing and I appreciate you using your skills to help me with this project. You are diligent, detailed, and have an abundance of creativity. You are a gift, and I am very thankful for your help with both books I have written.

Amanda McMullen – I am so thankful the Lord has connected us through our mutual friend, Julie Dixon. You have been a huge blessing in my life and I so appreciate your help during the editing process. Thank you for using your God-given gifts to aid me in book writing. You have a beautiful heart, and I am so grateful God placed you in my life.

Meredith Knox – Thank you so much for helping me with the forward of this book. You have a natural gift of creativity and your passion for Jesus exudes in all you do. Your words are inspirational and the way you communicate the Gospel message is powerful and applicable. Thank you for sharing your God-given talents within this project!

Clayton and Shanie King – Thank you both for your contribution and encouragement within the book writing process. Your words are so thoughtful and intentional. I appreciate the ways you seek to pour the love of Jesus into others with eagerness and joy.

Chris Wilson – You have been such a blessing to me and my family over the past few years. Knowing you and connecting with the Dream Center has deepened my faith and expanded my knowledge of Scripture. I appreciate your kind words and I love your joyful, servant-minded spirit.

Pam Ross – Thank you for being a God-honoring mentor to me throughout my college years. I deeply admire your strong faith in the Lord and I am so thankful or all your support over the years I have attended Anderson University.

Thank you to all who have helped in both big and small ways throughout this project. This book would not have been completed without the prayers, encouragement, and guidance along the way from friends and family members. Thank you to everyone who has supported me throughout my writing journey.

Also, thank you to the friends and family members that have demonstrated the fruit of the Spirit on a consistent basis. Observing the fruit of the Spirit within believers is one of the most tangible and effective ways God has helped me understand the fruit of the Spirit. The "Fruit Pursuit" would not have been possible without your example of faith in the Lord.

About the Author

Hannah Beth Brown is a recent graduate of Anderson University where she studied Christian Studies and Human Development and Family Studies. She has really enjoyed learning more about God and His people through her studies in college. Throughout her time at Anderson University, Hannah Beth has loved making new friends, learning in the classroom, and serving the community. Hannah Beth has enjoyed plugging into church at New Spring and leading a Bible study at Anderson University called TRUTH. God has blessed Hannah Beth with incredible relationships and experiences in college and she is excited to discover what God has planned for her as she steps into adult life. She is thankful for the opportunity to continue to learn more about the Lord and His people as she begins working as the Administrative Coordinator at the Dream Center in Easley, S.C. Hannah Beth is eager to step into this new season of life as she relies on God's wisdom to direct her path. Hannah Beth was excited to write her first book, "Ready, Set, Grow," and is thankful God led her to write her second book, "Fruit Pursuit," while in college. Please join Hannah Beth on this lifelong "Fruit Pursuit" journey!

I'd love to hear from you!
Please feel free to reach out at hannahbethbrownga@gmail.com.

– *Hannah Beth Brown*

Also by Hannah Beth Brown

A 52 WEEK
DEVOTIONAL FOR TEENS

"Ready, Set, Grow" was designed for YOU! This book includes fifty-two weekly devotionals to help you learn more about Christ. Each devotional is composed of three main parts: "Ready," "Set," and "Grow."

READY

"READY" is defined as, "to *prepare* someone or something for an activity or purpose." This section of the devotional includes a personal story and message that should prepare you to absorb His truths and act upon them.

SET

"SET" is defined as "to put, lay, or stand something in a specified place or *position*." This portion of the devotion contains multiple scripture verses. Scripture allows us to understand God's story and our position as His most treasured and beloved children.

GROW

"GROW" is "to progress to *maturity*." The last portion of each devotion includes a personal challenge or activity that is intended to mature your faith through intentional actions.

I chose to write a devotion that was weekly rather than daily for a very important reason. My prayer is that you would marinate on the contents of each devotion all week, reflecting on the story, memorizing the scriptures, and engaging in the suggested activities. Colossians 2:6-7 says, "Therefore, as you received Christ Jesus the Lord, so walk in him, rooted and built up in him and established in the faith, just as you were taught, abounding in thanksgiving."

My only goal in writing "Ready, Set, Grow" is to magnify the name of Christ. My prayer is that this book would allow you to draw nearer to Christ and learn more of His magnificent character and unending love. 1 Corinthians 2:9 says, "No eye has seen, no ear has heard, and no mind has imagined what God has prepared for those who love Him." God has big plans for you, so without further ado, Ready...Set...Grow!

Available on Amazon and other online vendors.

www.ingramcontent.com/pod-product-compliance
Ingram Content Group UK Ltd.
Pitfield, Milton Keynes, MK11 3LW, UK
UKHW061223180426
11947UKWH00027B/1996